The Other S~~ide~~

of Sales

An insider reveals the secrets
to dealing with professional buyers

COLOFON

Taste of Life boeken by Linda Baart concepts
www.tasteoflifeboeken.nl

Design: studio SIEN
ISBN 9789492744043

THIS BOOK IS DEDICATED TO FEMKE, THIJS AND FLOORTJE

Words cannot describe…

To Colly,

It's a pleasure meeting you. your background and experience makes me realize how much I still have to learn. Hopefully, I can return that favor with this book. Enjoy!

All the best, Mark

Table of contents

Preface

CHANGE EVERYTHING YOU THOUGHT YOU KNEW ABOUT SELLING TO PROFESSIONAL BUYERS

Wow! This book is a tough one. If you are in sales and think you 'understand the customer', can 'handle objections' or even 'reach the decision maker', think again. I dare you to read this book.

Mark is a real-life senior buyer who is literally a gamekeeper turned poacher. You can forget your scientific selling, hierarchies of need and all the rest of that mumbo jumbo because this guy knows the awful truth about professional buyers.

He reveals how much power a buyer has and hasn't got. He shows how going too far up the greasy pole can actually be counter-productive.

You may just be too insignificant for the Chief Procurement Officer to bother with (I told you it was tough). But Mark reveals the buyers' most guarded secrets and the book will guide you to the perfect sale through a series of searching questions. No fancy sales science or gimmicky persuasion techniques, but the raw facts that make professional buyers buy.

Are you dealing with dogs or cash cows? To find out and to upscale your sales career forever, you have to read this book.

If you are a senior sales professional, a key account manager or sales director working in a business to business environment, this book could change your life.

GEOFF BURCH

Geoff is an internationally renowned sales expert and the author of six bestselling books including the iconic 'Resistance is Useless', possibly the world's most popular book on sales.

1. Introduction

1.1 WHY DO YOU NEED A PLAN?

Buyers can be extremely annoying. Trust me, I have been one for over 15 years. Not all of them, of course, but there are always a few that you just can't seem to get your head around. You feel they have control over the relationship and that you should feel grateful just to do business with them. That sucks because <u>you</u> want to be in control, not them.

The real problem is that buyers have grown more powerful over time. The procurement function has undergone serious professionalisation and you simply can't get away with a good sales story like you could have in the past. This means it is time to focus on a new strategic plan of action. One that will give you inspiring insights to deal with the worst types of buyers. If only you knew what was going on inside their heads. If only you knew what pressure(s) they were under. For once, wouldn't you love to beat them at the negotiation table? Or perhaps know how to use all the information at your disposal to create a mutually sustainable relationship? Believe me when I say that you can make it happen. All you need to do is to get into the mind of a buyer.

This book is intended for all sales professionals who deal with professional buyers on a regular basis and sometimes feel they are losing out in the relationship. It's a step-by-step guide on your journey from good to great at sales. Unlike most other books, this book will be highly confrontational and filled with critical questions. They can be easily identified throughout the book as they are *highlighted in italic* and begin with '*Q*'.

Go to https://roi-10.com/the-other-side-of-sales/ to receive a free PDF document with all questions for easy use throughout the book. The more effort you put in, the better your results will be. Nobody else is going to change the situation for you; the power is in your hands.

So, step out of your comfort zone and step into the mysterious world of buyers. It is one they have kept closed for too long. All its secrets are about to be revealed.

1.2 BUYERS AND SELLERS

The first recorded profession in history wasn't a king, a slaver or a warrior. It was actually a business man. In Mesopotamia a 5,000-year-old clay tablet was found which appears to record some kind of business deal. In his book 'Sapiens', Yuval Noah Harari states that the most probable reading of this tablet is: 'A total of 29,086 measures of barley were received over the course of 37 months. Signed, Kushim.'

Figure 1.1 © The Schøyen Collection, Oslo and London

http://www.schoyencollection.com/24-smaller-collections/wine-beer/ms-1717-beer-inanna-uruk

From this perspective, it seems that doing business is the second oldest profession in the world. It also means buyers and sellers have been around for over 5,000 years. You might expect the game of buying and selling would be perfect by now, but that is far from the truth. Still today, we struggle to truly understand the other party. How wonderful would it be that after so many millennia someone finally shows up to help close that gap? Well, all I can say is: 'Here you go, enjoy the read'.

2. First things first

2.1 PERSPECTIVE

There is this one picture that I just cannot seem to let go of. I am somehow drawn to it every time I look at it. The reason is that it is simplistic yet insightful. It's funny and sad at the same time. Most importantly, I can imagine myself being both of these people.

Figure 2.1 Different perspectives on an essentially similar situation

In the picture, both people are in the exact same situation, although they both think the other is better off. It's all a matter of perspective. We tend to stay stuck inside our own head and forget that others might have a different view of the situation. It's a good reminder that what we might think is important may be completely different for others. The best way to understand an other party's perspective is actually not that difficult; all you need to do is ask and listen.

> Throughout my career, I have had thousands of interactions with key account managers, sales directors, and the like. Surprisingly, I received the following question only once during my entire career:
>
> 'Mark, what are your exact objectives this year?'
>
> I thought it was such a powerful question that I still remember who asked it and where I was at the time. It's a shame that this question is not raised more often. It could hold incredible power if a buyer was invited to tell you their objectives and you could use that information to help the buyer achieve these objectives.

Neither buyers nor sellers are necessarily wrong in any given situation, they just have their own points of reference and perspective. This means you have to put in some effort to find out what that is. Remember that, as a seller, you only see part of the procurement process; typically, just the interactions you have with the buyer, which are often biased by your own perspective. In reality, there is much more to it since buyers interact with a variety of stakeholders that influence their objectives and decisions.

I was once involved in a negotiation between a manufacturer and a retailer. For the new contract year, the manufacturer wanted to raise prices by 3% driven by increases in raw material prices. The retailer, on the other hand, was expecting a price decrease of 6,5% driven by changing market conditions.

Neither party was wrong in this case, they simply had different underlying data and therefore a different perspective. The first step for both parties to come to an agreement was to understand the other party's point of view. Although it wasn't easy accepting that the other party was also right, it definitely benefited the rest of negotiation.

By understanding their perspective, and with a little bit of creativity, you enter into a world of possibilities. Rather than being price focused, for example, there may be other potential benefits for you and, if you wish, your customer too. Throughout the rest of the book, you will be encouraged to think about both parties' positions. The reason is simple: you cannot think in isolation if you want to get the most out of the relationship with your customer.

2.2 YOUR CHALLENGE

With all of that in mind, it's now time to think about your individual challenge. While you read the previous paragraphs, what was the name of the customer that had you thinking:

'If only I knew how to deal with customer x'

That's it. That's the one we will be focusing on throughout this book.

▶ *Q01. What customer do you have in mind? Which person/buyer in particular? (from now on this person is called customer x)*

Additionally, it's important to think about and understand why this currently is a problem.

▶ *Q02. What is the specific challenge you have with them? What issues do you keep running into with customer x?*

Thirdly, it's crucial to define where you want to be at the end of your journey.

▶ *Q03. What do you want to learn or understand about customer x? What does success look like for you?*

To help you achieve your objectives, we will continue to share the perspective of a buyer and how that relates to you as a seller throughout this book. By switching back and forth, you will gain different tools to help you overcome any current and future challenge with your customers.

2.3 THE VISION FOR SUCCESS

Unfortunately, I often experience the inferior position that sales professionals put themselves in. They almost automatically assume they are at the mercy of buyers to be awarded business. I believe this has been part of an evolutionary process driven by a:

Learning opportunity

When I coached sales and buying professionals, I asked two specific questions to both and often got two different answers. These questions are the following:

1. Did you ever practice with your manager or with a peer before going into negotiation?
2. Did you ever have your manager or a peer present at a negotiation you were leading?

The answer from buyers would typically be 'YES', since they are actively looking for feedback from people more experienced than they are to learn from. The answer from sales people would typically be 'NO', since they are often afraid to show weakness to peers or senior people believing it would reflect badly on them. The net result is that buyers have gotten so much better at the negotiation game over the years, and it shows. Buyers are typically in control of the relationship with their suppliers.

In helping sales professionals to step up, I see a world where there is an equal playing field for buyers and sellers to operate in. There is genuinely so much more fun and enjoyment in balance than in the powerplay we too often see these days.

3. Let's agree on this

To ensure we start off on the right foot, we need to have a common understanding of some of the definitions around buying and selling.

3.1 WHAT'S IN A NAME?

You will have heard many different job titles for procurement professionals, such as:

buyer, strategic sourcing manager, buying manager, strategic buyer, procurement manager, purchasing director, category leader global strategic sourcing, ... and any possible variation on this

Essentially, what's in a name? While they will all have different roles to play such as executing strategies, running tenders, doing cost optimisation projects, etc., but when it concerns the relationship with you it comes down to the same thing:

They are sitting on the other side of the negotiating table

For ease, the term 'buyer' will be used throughout this book. The simple reason is that this is what they are paid to do. The same applies for the term 'seller'.

Additionally, you'll find names such as 'supplier' and 'customer'. A customer is a buyer and a supplier is a seller.

You will also come across the words 'procurement' and 'purchasing'. These terms are often used interchangeably, however, purchasing deals with the actual buying of a product or service whereas procurement means to deal with the entire process around it. Purchasing is therefore only one part of the procurement process.

3.2 THE MARKET

The best definition of a market is the following:

'A market is a medium that allows buyers and sellers of a specific good or service to interact in order to facilitate an exchange.'

That means that a market contains four key elements:
1. **Medium:** traditionally a physical place such as a bazaar or shopping center; nowadays also a virtual space such as eBay or a stock exchange.
2. **Buyers and sellers:** a minimum of two parties needs to be involved.
3. **Specific good or service:** what the seller wants to sell and the buyer wants to buy.
4. **Facilitate an exchange:** there needs to be grounds for the two parties to come to an agreement.

It's important to understand the market from a buyer's perspective because if you do, you'll know exactly who your competitors are and you can therefore assess the power you have in the relationship.

A chocolate manufacturer in Nigeria needed coarse white sugar (high granularity and non-industry standard) for the manufacturing of its products. Due to high temperatures and humidity, industry standard sugar would clump and clog the pipes in the factory, causing significant delays. This meant that the manufacturer could only source from a local supplier since they were the only ones capable of delivering the required specifications.

One day, the supplier informed the manufacturer that they had to stop the supply of the coarse sugar due to maintenance work in their factory. This left the manufacturer with few options. A project team was created consisting of quality & food safety professionals, engineers, factory operators and procurement specialists to deal with the challenge. Eventually they came up with a feasible solution to move to industry standard sugar. From that point onward, all four variables changed:

1. **Medium:** the marketplace changed from local sourcing to a global market place.
2. **Buyers and sellers:** from one seller to many potential sellers.
3. **Specific good or service:** the product changed from customer-specific to industry standard sugar.
4. **Facilitate an exchange:** the grounds for agreement became very favourable for the buyer.

The result was that the supplier lost their entire business with this manufacturer. If they would have pre-empted this issue by building stock or any other viable solution, they would still be in business with the manufacturer today.

Within one industry, a company can operate in multiple markets. A car dealer, for example, can be active in one or more of the following markets:

✓ Selling new cars
✓ Selling used cars
✓ Leasing cars
✓ Maintenance and repairs

Even though it's the same industry, each market is different for the simple reason that they each have different competitors and/or customers.

▶ *Q04. For the product or service that you sell to customer x, is the market you operate in global, regional or local?*
▶ *Q05. Roughly, how many buyers and sellers are active in this market?*

4. The buyer's world

When a sales person calls a buyer 'bad', 'ok' or 'good', it's probably a way of saying that buyers are respectively negotiating based on price, cost or value. Yes, sure, there are still buyers that can be classified as one-trick ponies. However, it could be damaging to assume that this is the case for every buyer you meet. The modern buyer is able to apply different tools depending on the situation they are in.

Since procurement is only one of many functions in an organisation, it's important to understand what really makes a buyer tick by looking at the bigger picture. Their behaviour can be driven by personal preference. However, it's more likely their objectives are determined by a top-down approach within their organisation.

4.1 COMPANY EXPECTATIONS

From a holistic company perspective, you could argue that the way a buyer is expected to approach the market is based on the position of its products in the BCG-matrix. The BCG-matrix was developed by the Boston Consulting Group in the 1970s and continues to be one of the most popular tools for portfolio analysis.

Relative Market Share

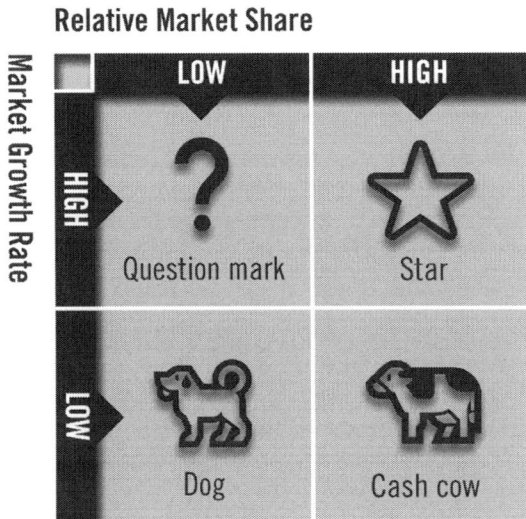

Figure 4.1 BCG-matrix

On the vertical axis of the matrix you'll find market growth rate, which explains the attractiveness of the industry from a growth perspective. The horizontal axis shows the relative market share which determines the competitive position of an organisation within the industry. Combined, there are four different stages in the BCG-matrix:

1. **Question mark:** low market share and high market growth. This is typically the start of the life cycle; procurement is expected to support the company's growth ambitions; hence the focus will be on anything that will help grow the relative market share and turn it into a star.
2. **Star:** high market share and high market growth. This means that there is a 'make it happen' mentality. Buyers would seek partnerships with reliable suppliers. Price is less of an issue here so long as supply security and quality are guaranteed.
3. **Cash Cow:** high market share and low market growth. Procurement will be focused on cost reduction. This is where companies would like to maximise their profits so they can invest in question marks or stars. Hence, procurement will be involved in running tenders and other cost-cutting exercises.

4. **Dog:** low market share and low market growth. This is the end of the life-cycle. The only way to stay in the market is by being price-leader, which means procurement will be focused on price reduction. Expect tough negotiations here.

There are typically two routes a product can follow through the BCG-matrix:

1. **A successful product:** Question mark –> star –> cash cow –> dog
    A new innovation typically starts with a low market share and high growth potential (question mark). When it materialises, market share grows (star) to a point where growth potential declines at high market share (cash cow). Finally, towards the end of the life cycle, newer and better products emerge leading to low market share and low growth potential of the original product (dog).
2. **An unsuccessful product:** Question mark –> dog
    A new innovation typically starts with a low market share and high growth potential (question mark). If unsuccessful, growth potential declines (dog).

As a rule of thumb, all businesses can do without dogs, although these products can be maintained in a portfolio for strategic reasons.

One industry that truly understands how the BCG-matrix works is the pharmaceutical industry. They are aware that they need a good spread of cash cows, stars and question marks in their portfolios. In their business, new product development processes can take up to 25 years or longer, so they need cash cows and stars to fund and fuel their question marks. Pharmaceutical companies without questions marks will not survive in the long term and therefore only have two options: acquire or be acquired.

Note that a company can have multiple products in different stages of the BCG-matrix. This means there is no one-size-fits-all approach with regard to how procurement approaches the market. That said, as a guiding principle, you can place the entire company into one of the four boxes of the BCG-matrix to determine the company-wide approach to procurement.

▶ *Q06. How would you classify the products or services that customer x is selling to their customers, according to the BCG-matrix?*
▶ *Q07. Given the classification, what procurement approach fits best? Does this fit with how customer x approaches you?*

4.2 PROCUREMENT MATURITY

The level at which a procurement organisation operates determines its maturity. The higher on the pyramid, the more mature it is. Note that this can be driven by the company's position in the BCG-matrix, however it can also be determined by the intrinsic level of professionalism in the procurement organisation.

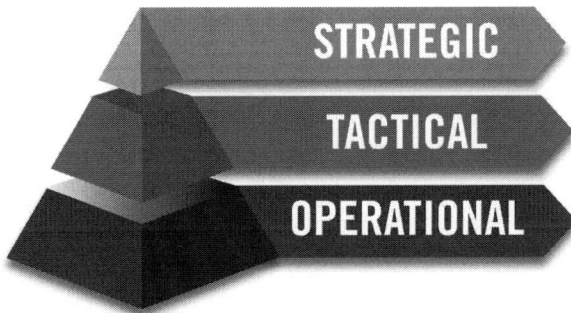

Figure 4.2 Procurement maturity pyramid (adapted from Van Weele (2000))

STRATEGIC (1 YEAR+)

Companies operating at this level are using internal and external data points to create a multi-year strategy including an execution plan. Less than 20% of companies operate at this level, which is a shame since this is where procurement can achieve the highest level of value. This includes focus areas such as long-term partnerships, supplier performance management, tendering, supplier development, supplier enabled innovation and a whole lot more.

TACTICAL (1 MONTH – 1 YEAR)

Companies operating at this level are using a five-step routine that they execute. They are:

1. Specifying their needs
2. Selecting suppliers to source from
3. Defining their purchasing approach
4. Negotiating the deal
5. Contracting their business

An estimated 50% of companies operate at a tactical level. If your customer is one of them, then it's highly likely that you will be going through rigorous selection and tender processes. Typically, these customers fail to see the whole spectrum of procurement and are focused on delivering short-term (maximum 1 year) results. Companies operating at strategic level also operate at tactical level, so if you're taking part in a tender, it could mean you are working with a company operating at either.

OPERATIONAL (0 - 1 MONTH)

Companies operating at this level are focused on ordering their materials, ensuring collection, correct invoicing and payment and managing supplier performance. All companies are operational, since this is what keeps the business going; roughly 30% only operate at this level. If your customer is one of them, then there is no real fear of losing your business with them so long as you keep them satisfied in terms of service, quality and, to a lesser extent, cost. This is how a lot of business was done in the past.

SO, WHAT DOES THAT MEAN FOR YOU?

Typically, the highest level of frustration for a sales professional sits with companies operating at a tactical level only. They are running tenders like well-oiled machines as if they do nothing else. The difference with strategic procurement teams is that they run tenders as part of a broader plan. Depending on the situation, they remain flexible to see value in other elements of cooperation.

To understand your position, it's important to know on which level your customer is operating since it defines the level of professionalism you are dealing with.

▶ *Q08. Is customer x operating at a strategic, tactical or operational level? How can you tell?*

4.3 THE IMPORTANCE OF PROCUREMENT

We have now assessed the way buyers' objectives are set and how that drives behaviour. However, it's also important to understand the relative position of procurement in an organisation. When dealing with buyers, we almost automatically assume they have a lot of power in the relationship. However, a critical question that needs answering remains:

How powerful do you think a buyer is within their own organisation?

Of course, buyers want you to assume that they are powerful internally because it helps to put pressure on to you, but this isn't necessarily the case. Let's take a look at three perspectives to analyse this in more detail.

4.3.1 PERSPECTIVE 1 - HIERARCHY

Even though buyers can come across as the ultimate source of power in negotiations, their reporting lines suggest otherwise. Normally buyers report into a Chief Procurement Officer (CPO) and in its turn, the three most common reporting lines for CPO's are:

1. Chief Financial Officer (CFO) – The person responsible for overseeing the financial activities of an entire company.
2. Chief Operational Officer (COO) – The person responsible for managing the company's day-to-day operations.
3. Chief Executive Officer (CEO) – The person responsible for overseeing the activities of an entire company.

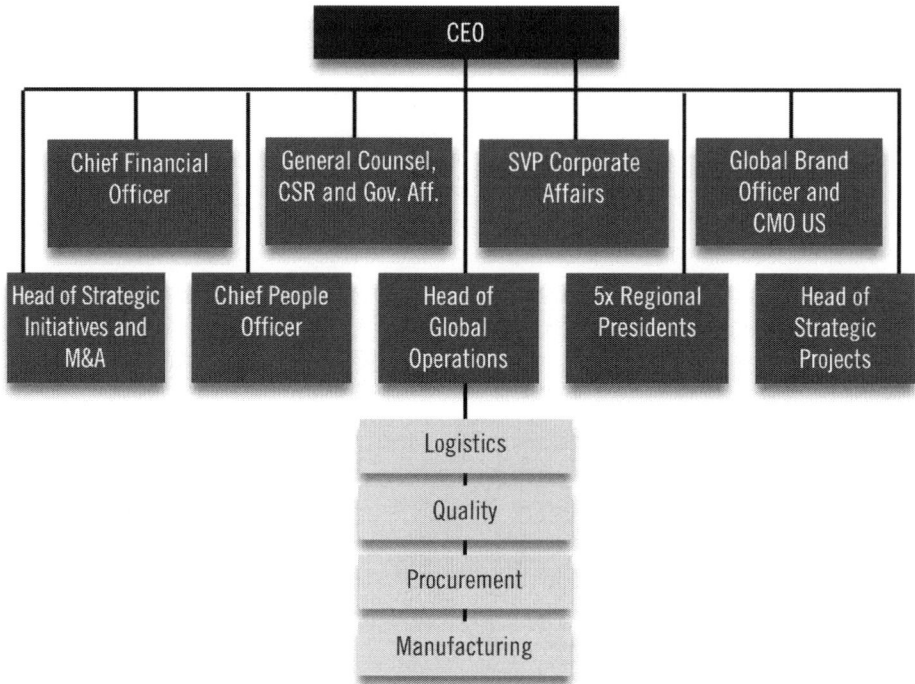

Figure 4.3 Organisation chart of the Kraft Heinz company 2019 (shortened job titles). Procurement reporting into Head of Global Operations (COO). For full description see: http://ir.kraftheinzcompany.com/company-profile/management

Understanding the reporting line helps you to understand each division's functional objectives, assuming they are cascaded down to the level of individual objectives.

REPORTING INTO THE CFO

My personal experience has shown that CFOs who have a CPO reporting into them, are often unaware of the exact dealings of their procurement teams. The reason for this is that finance constitutes a large portion of their responsibilities and this is where most of their focus lies. Indirectly, this means they give great levels of responsibility to CPOs.

For CFOs that are actively involved in procurement, the key objective is to make sure that financials such as the Balance Sheet, Cash-Flow Statement and Profit & Loss Statement (P&L) are in good shape. From this perspective, the most important impact buyers have is by managing:

✓ Costs through better buying (mainly impacting the P&L Statement)
✓ Cash through stock management and payment terms (mainly impacting the Balance Sheet and Cash-Flow Statement)

It goes without saying that buyers can have a direct or indirect impact on other elements of the three financial statements mentioned above.

REPORTING INTO THE COO

Procurement teams that report into the COO will typically experience a certain level of tension because their objectives balance between cost and service. The COO's primary focus will be on managing day-to-day activities, so buyers reporting into COOs will be instructed to focus on delivering excellent service before focusing on costs. I'll explain later why this is actually a good decision.

REPORTING INTO THE CEO

Roughly 25% of companies have a CPO reporting into the CEO. They will typically see a more balanced approach to procurement with a focus on multiple objectives such as cost, cash, service, quality, innovation and more. A true CEO will see the wide spectrum of business activities and departments and will aim to build strong connections with respect to each functional contribution.

In world-class organisations, procurement will be seen as one of the few departments with an extensive external network, hence a powerful source of external innovation capability that can help drive a company's growth agenda. This requires a strong link between all functions of an organisation, specifically the internal relationship between sales/marketing and procurement.

IN SUMMARY

The reporting line of the procurement function will clarify its objectives at the negotiation table. In all instances, cost and cash will be important, however the focus on other objectives often depends on the hierarchical structure of the organisation.

▶ *Q09. Do you know what reporting line structure customer x has?*
   CFO, COO, CEO or other?
▶ *Q10. As a result, what functional objectives might customer x have?*

4.3.2 PERSPECTIVE 2 – THE SUPPLY CHAIN

If we look at procurement from a supply chain perspective, we can use the following sentence explaining a company's view of it:

'you need to <u>buy</u> it well,
so you can <u>make</u> it well
and you can <u>sell</u> it well'

In a simple schematic overview, it looks much like this:

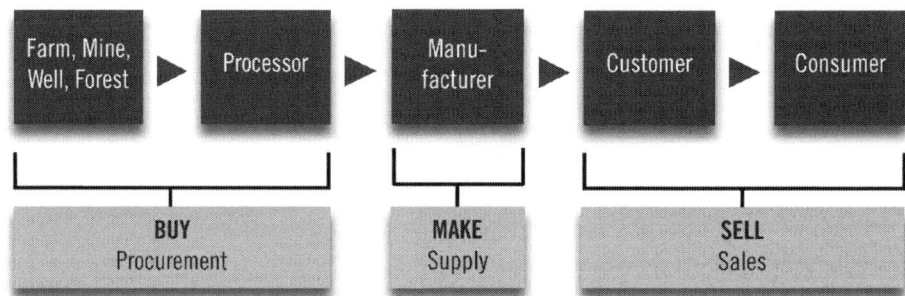

Figure 4.4 Schematic overview of a traditional supply chain

This means that procurement is at the start of every supply chain. Buyers buy materials needed to manufacture products that can be sold to customers and consumers. This seems like it would imply that it holds an important position at the start of the process. However, the reality is that companies are often more focused on the last part of the supply chain: sales! This actually makes complete sense.

There are only a few companies in this world who don't focus on growing their business, and that is likely because they don't need to. For every other company, growth through increased sales is considered the number one objective. All you need to do is read through several annual business reports to see this for yourself. From that rationale, procurement is merely a service function to supply, which in turn is a service function to sales. Sales will tell supply what they need to manufacture and supply will tell procurement what to buy so they can manufacture it.

From a communication perspective, this means that procurement will only have access to sales through supply, unless of course there is an organisational shortcut. In reality, and specifically in large organisations, the communication line between sales and procurement is limited or even non-existent. If there would be a communication line, a typical comment from a sales person to a buyer could look like this:

'If we don't sell anything, your job wouldn't exist'

Bearing in mind that most companies are sales-driven organisations, this means that the power of the procurement function is limited for the simple reason that procurement is on the far end of the supply chain. So, for all you sales professional out there: you are more important inside your own organisation than your buying counterpart is in theirs.

Sales beats procurement in any organisation

Feels good, right? Hopefully, that gives you added confidence going into negotiations next time.

4.3.3 PERSPECTIVE 3 – THE PROFIT & LOSS STATEMENT

All business leaders are accountable for the financial results of their business. A Profit & Loss Statement (P&L) is a vital tool for assessing the financial wellbeing of an organisation. In reality, most P&Ls will be significantly more complex, however for simplicity's sake, let's examine the most basic version of it:

```
+ Sales
- Cost of Goods Sold
= Gross profit
- Overhead
= Net profit
```

Figure 4.5 Example of a P&L statement

The impact of the procurement team can be found in both 'cost of goods sold' for the sourcing of raw materials, packaging and production, as well as in the 'overhead', which includes all other expenses like media, marketing, logistics and services. For a typical manufacturing business, this means that anywhere between 50-80% of the sales value is bought. You can see that the impact of procurement on business results is very high. If you think about it in a simplified manner, it's actually pretty straightforward:

Every dollar saved by procurement goes straight to the bottom line of the P&L

Every dollar saved is a dollar net profit. Given that perspective, you'd have to agree that this has quite an impact, right? Well, not completely, since profit is actually overrated in today's business environment. I'm not saying it's not important, but there are certain other things that should take priority over profit. Here are two stories that illustrate this well.

LIVE BREAKING NEWS

2018 Interrupted Supply Chain
Cost: several millions GB Pounds

A Fast-Food chain changed service provider for its deliveries of frozen products in the UK. Due to a variety of reasons several hundreds of restaurants ran out of stock. As a result, the Fast-Food chain reverted back to its previous supplier to secure the supply of frozen products to its restaurants. They saw a 2% reduction in same-store sales and a 5% operating profit decline in the first quarter.

Figure 4.6 Interrupted Supply Chain in the UK

With regard to the Fast-Food chain, here is one way it could have gone: A cross-functional team, led by a buyer, decided to switch suppliers driven by a savings opportunity. With the transition to the new supplier, some things didn't quite work out well. The outcome was that one of three restaurants closed due to non-supply of ingredients (frozen products). Can you imagine the conversation between the CEO and that particular buyer? I'm guessing it went something like this:

'#@$%@, I want you to switch back to the old supplier immediately and get compensation from the new supplier for the mess they have created'

Not particularly a position of power from the buyer's perspective if you ask me.

LIVE BREAKING NEWS

2013 Airbags
Cost: 24 billion USD >20 deaths

Known as the biggest recall in history. Faulty air-bag inflators made by a now-bankrupt company were used by virtually every major automaker on the planet. The issue: the inflators can explode and eject a shrapnel-like material that has been linked to at least 20 deaths. Globally, 100 million inflators are under recall. Regulators say it could take until 2023 to recall and fix every vehicle with a faulty air bag.

Figure 4.7 Airbags recall

In this example, the supply of faulty airbags led to the biggest recall ever recorded, costing billions of dollars and, more importantly, over 20 lives. Can you imagine the cost and reputation impact on a car manufacturer that has to recall millions of cars? Unimaginable! How do you think the conversation went between the CEO and the airbags buyer? Again, I'm guessing it was something along the lines of:

'OMG, what have we done? We need to switch to a new supplier immediately and think about a plan of action how we are going to manage the situation we are in'

Here, the buyer's objectives are determined by the business objectives. This is once again not a particularly powerful position from a buyer's perspective. As you can see, in both examples, quality and service impacted sales and reputation. Reputation is the factor which determines future sales. Therefore, the significance of sales is always greater than the advantage of lower cost.

From a P&L perspective, lower sales value means lower sales value and lower profits. Higher costs just mean lower profits. This makes it crystal clear:

Costs are always less important than service and quality

4.4 THE REAL STORY

You might read that the influence of procurement is growing and that they are becoming more and more professional. Even though there is an element of truth in there, procurement will rarely be seen as the priority function in any business. Of course, there is a place for procurement since they help to ensure short- and long-term profitability, act as an enabler for investments by generating cash and perhaps even fuel innovation. Nevertheless, no matter what perspective you take (hierarchy, supply chain or P&L), procurement is typically seen as an executive function:

✓ **Delivering the lowest costs against good quality and service**
✓ **Generating cash by increasing payment terms & stock level management**

So, whenever you find yourself at the negotiation table with a buyer, remember the iceberg analogy: the biggest part of the iceberg is below sea level and is often difficult to see.

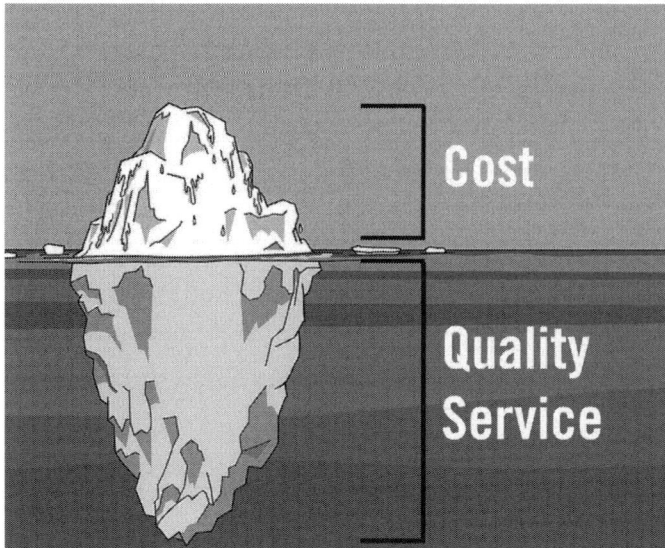

Figure 4.8 Buyer's objectives you typically see and don't see when negotiating

In procurement, it's the same because underneath the cost negotiations lies another interesting layer to behold, one that buyers try to protect at all...costs.

- ▶ *Q11. What business priorities does the company of customer x have?*
- ▶ *Q12 Given those priorities, how much power do you think the buyer has inside their own organisation?*
- ▶ *Q13. How can you use their business priorities to influence customer x?*

5. The principles of negotiation

Even though you likely have plenty of sales and negotiation experience yourself, it never hurts to understand why you have been successful throughout your career. I'm sure you have some negotiation tricks that work well for you, but do you know why they work? I'll bet you that in some way, shape or form, they are connected to one or more of the three fundamental principles of negotiation: satisfaction, level of comfort and power.

5.1 SATISFACTION

Negotiation is all about satisfaction in the same way winning a game is. In both cases, you will feel more satisfied when your win is the result of your tactical or strategic decisions.

Satisfaction can best be defined as a pleasant feeling that you get when you receive something you wanted, or when you have done something you wanted to do. While that pleasant feeling suggests something emotional, there is actually a semi-mathematical formula that explains satisfaction best:

Satisfaction = Reality -/- Expectations

Here's how that works in practice:

SCENARIO 1:

You are working as an account manager in the software industry. It is the end of December and the year has been going rather well. Your expectation is that you will receive a bonus of $20,000. Your boss comes over to tell you that sales have been disappointing toward the end of the year and that your bonus pay out will be $10,000. On a scale of one (very dissatisfied) to ten (very satisfied), how satisfied would you feel?

SCENARIO 2:

You are working as an account manager in the software industry. It is the end of December and the year has been going rather poorly. Your expectation is that you will receive a bonus of $5,000. Your boss comes over to tell you that sales have been promising toward the end of the year and that your bonus pay out will be $10,000. On a scale from one (very dissatisfied) to ten (very satisfied), how satisfied would you feel?

It's highly likely that the number for scenario 1 is lower than for scenario 2, which is fascinating since the actual result of your bonus is exactly the same. The only difference between both situations are your expectations going in.

In the first scenario:
satisfaction = 10,000 (reality) − 20,000 (expectations)
satisfaction = −10,000

In the second scenario:
satisfaction = 10,000 (reality) − 5,000 (expectations)
satisfaction = +5,000

The same logic applies in negotiations. It is key to ensure the other party is satisfied with the result. If they are not, they will look for ways to undo the deal or will leave the negotiation with a negative feeling. This potentially impacts your future sales. In the end, it's about your satisfaction as well as the satisfaction of the other party.

5.1.1 MANAGING EXPECTATIONS

You now understand why satisfaction is important. The next step is to focus on how to increase the satisfaction of the other party. In order to do that, you have two options:

1. Create a better reality for the other party, which essentially means giving them what they want, or
2. Lowering their expectations. This is about making the other party believe that their expectations weren't realistic to begin with.

Ideally, you won't be giving the other party what they want, since this leaves you with little or no satisfaction, so the trick is to focus on lowering their expectations instead (option 2). The best way to do this, is by understanding the pressures of the other party. Let's have a look at two different scenarios that illustrate the importance of managing expectations:

You're interested in buying a car that's for sale for $10,000. The car is in good condition. You walk up to the salesperson and start the following conversation:

You: 'I'm interested in this car, are you willing to sell it for $8,000?'
Salesperson: 'Yes, we've got a deal!'

In this situation, all you'll probably be thinking is that you should have made a lower proposal. As soon as the salesperson said yes, your initial expectations shifted immediately. Here's why that makes sense:

People value more what they have to fight for. The harder the fight, the more they value the outcome.

In this case, there wasn't much of a fight since the other party accepted quickly, leaving you with little to no satisfaction.

Now imagine this scenario:

You're interested in buying a car that's for sale for $10,000. The car is in good condition. You walk up to the salesperson and start the following conversation:

You:	'I'm interested in this car, are you willing to sell it for $8,000?'
Salesperson:	'Thank you for your offer. Unfortunately, I won't be able to do that, however I am willing to sell you this magnificent car for $9,500.'
You:	'Can we do $8,500?'
Salesperson:	'I can go as low as $9,200.'
You:	'$8,800?'
Salesperson:	'Let's agree on $9,000 and you are the proud owner of a fantastic car.'
You:	'Deal!'

Even though you pay more in the second scenario ($9,000) than in the first scenario ($8,000), you feel more satisfied with the outcome. Fascinating if you think about it, isn't it? The reason for this, from a psychological perspective, is that you feel you have influenced the other party to move to your position. Since you feel you made it happen, you now feel responsible for the result. This means you are more likely to live up to the agreement as well.

In summary, by going through the ritual of back and forth proposing, you influence the expectations of the other party. As a result, they will feel more satisfied with the outcome because they fought for it. This means there needs to be room to negotiate and therefore it's appropriate to open higher than where you want to end up. This leaves you with space to negotiate for the simple reason to provide satisfaction to the other party. That also means that you should never accept the first offer, since that gives the other party little satisfaction. You now know you should focus on managing their expectations by making them fight for it.

5.2 COMFORT

We love feeling comfortable and, in all fairness, it's not a bad place to be. However, we also need to realise that this is not where the magic happens. This is the 'easy sailing territory' where you don't really push the boundaries. The same applies in negotiations. It's important to accept that negotiations are almost always uncomfortable. Not just for you, also for the other party.

When you feel uncomfortable, your body produces adrenaline resulting in an enhanced level of concentration and focus. This is actually useful during negotiations and will help get you a better result than if you were comfortable.

If you were completely stressed out during negotiations, you would be emotional and unable to apply logic. I am not saying emotions are bad in negotiations, they can be extremely powerful, however uncontrolled emotions are very destructive. When you're stressed out, your emotions are more difficult to control.

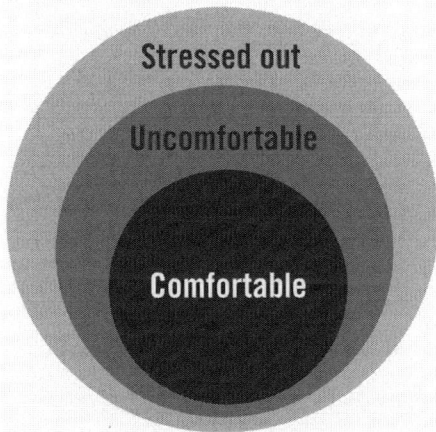

Figure 5.1 The 3 levels of comfort in negotiations

I have seen it happen once during my career: a supplier (a middle-aged man) bursting into tears saying he would lose his job if he didn't secure the deal with me that day. I have seen many tactics in my life, but a grown man crying is pretty rare. If it actually was a tactic, that man deserves an Oscar®. I was so flabbergasted that I can't even remember whether I awarded him the business or not.

If we know that almost all negotiations are uncomfortable, what does that mean in practice? People do not typically like being uncomfortable, so they try to 'buy' back their comfort by giving the other party what they want. There are many ways to make the other party feel uncomfortable, ranging from subtle to extreme:

1. **Reciprocity.** People feel a sense of obligation to repay a perceived debt. Example: Many years ago, followers of the Hare Krishna-movement were handing out flowers to passersby at airports. People who accepted this seemingly free gift later on were asked to donate to the cause.

2. **Make them feel guilty.** This means giving the other party the feeling that they have done something wrong or that they have let you down. By making people feel guilty, they look for ways to make it up to you. Example: 'I have a feeling you don't appreciate all I do for you. I would really appreciate if you could do something for me now.'

3. **Silence.** Absence of sound makes people feel uncomfortable which encourages them to talk, give information or concede.
   Example: A: 'The minimum price I can sell this for is $20'
              B: [silence]....
              A: 'Ok, do we have a deal for $18?'

4. **Social pressure.** This is the use of group pressure to force decisions. Example: If you ask a group of 100 people, 'Who thinks the Eiffel Tower is located in Rome, Italy?', and 99 pre-instructed people raise their hands, there is a high likelihood that the 100th person will raise their hand too for the mere reason they feel uncomfortable standing alone.

5. **Physical disturbance.** The use of a variety of physical means to throw the other party off balance.
   Example: Sitting too close to the other party, lowering their seats or making them look into the sunlight during the negotiation.
6. **Personal attack.** Deliberately verbally attacking someone to destabilise the negotiation.
   Example: 'I have never ever worked with such an incompetent person like you during my entire life. You disgust me.'

Newton's third law states that for every action there is an equal and opposite reaction. The same applies in negotiations. An extreme approach such as a personal attack, will have a direct impact on the relationship with the other party, so be aware of the consequences of the approach you choose. I once experienced an unintended, yet classic example of the use of silence and social pressure.

We had monthly conference calls with our local procurement team of around 50 people hosted by our regional procurement Vice-President. In one instance, we had forgotten to book a meeting room and, by the time we realised, there was only one free room remaining.

We hurried to the room and suddenly an other man walks in holding a laptop and a cup of coffee, claiming to have booked the room. He looked at me for a response, as I was heading the department at the time, and I genuinely didn't know what to say. Instead, I stayed silent for what must have been about five seconds.

Imagine this person standing in the doorway with 50 people staring at him. These five seconds must have felt like five minutes, and before I knew it he followed up: 'But since there are so many of you, I'll see if I can find another room', and he left never to return. It was obvious he felt uncomfortable and he created a comfortable situation for himself by giving us the room and walking away.

This is what happens to all of us; we don't like feeling uncomfortable so we try to buy off the awkward feeling. In negotiations, this means giving the other party what they want. Goodbye money, hello comfort!

We need to learn to feel comfortable with being uncomfortable

5.3 POWER

Imagine a man walks into the room holding a gun in his hand while shouting:

'Get down on the floor with your hands behind your back'

Who of you would lie down on the floor? Unless you're trained for these circumstances, I'm pretty sure you'd obey immediately, right?

Imagine that you found out that the gun he is holding doesn't contain any bullets. Who would lie down now? Maybe some people would still feel intimidated, but I'm pretty sure fewer would listen to his demands than in the first scenario. You might even consider restraining him if you saw an opportunity to do so.

The difference between both situations is the difference between actual power and perceived power. Initially, the man had high perceived power because of the gun in his hand. Later you found out he had no actual power because he didn't have any bullets.

Actual power = the power you actually have
Perceived power = the power people think you have

Now, negotiations are always about <u>perceived</u> power. Even in situations when you have actual power, if the other party can make you believe they have more power, you will lose the negotiations.

Throughout my career, I have run dozens of tenders and I'm not afraid to admit that we were bloody good at it. A tender is a very powerful tool to create perceived power. When you are participating as a supplier, you never know exactly who your competitors are for each specification you bid on. Even if you are the only one able to provide a specific product or service, you never know for sure whether that is truly the case.

Buyers will protect this kind of information at all costs, and they will never tell you if competitors made a quote or not. Why? Because if they would, they would immediately lose power, which negatively impacts their negotiation position. They definitely don't want that. It's that simple!

As a seller you might assume that when your service, quality and prices are great, a customer has no reason to tender. That's not entirely true. They might not have a reason to leave, but the reason to tender is to put pressure on the relationship and to show power.

We very often use the terms 'buyer's market' and 'seller's market'; these are ways of saying who has more power in this specific market. Imagine the following two scenarios:

1. You want to buy a house that has been for sale for one day and there are six others interested in buying that exact same house, or
2. You want to buy a house that has been for sale for six months and nobody has shown any interest so far.

The perceived balance of power is quite clear in both cases.
A simple way for a buyer to find out how much power they actually have over you is by asking what your company's total revenue is. They can then easily calculate what percentage of business they would be to you by using their own

spend data. Even without asking you, this information is available through your annual reports. This is one more reason why you should have a good spread of customers you do business with.

A large internet-based hotel booking platform had a commercial disagreement with a large chain of hotels. The dispute was based on different contractual terms and conditions which resulted in the hotel chain losing over $1 million in profits. Obviously, the hotel chain wasn't pleased and summoned the owner of the booking platform to its headquarters in the United States.

Upon for arrival, the hotel chain had called a handful of lawyers to substantiate the legal basis of the claim in more detail. The owner of the booking platform came alone and listened to the other party's case. At the end he reached inside his jacket and said: 'You're absolutely right, here's a cheque worth $1 million.'

The other party looked surprised assuming they would have to put up a fight. As one person reached out to take the cheque, the owner revealed his winning argument: 'And if you take this cheque, we'll never book a hotel with you again.'

Now, that's the difference between perceived power and actual power. The hotel chain assumed they had perceived power whereas the owner had actual power. It was only when the owner explicitly expressed this to the hotel chain that he was able to align perceived power with his actual power and therefore win the negotiation. In negotiations, it is important to shift the perceived balance of power in your favour. Here are two questions to consider:

► *Q14. Think about the power balance between customer x and yourself. Who has actual power and who has perceived power?*
► *Q15. If you have no actual power, what can you do to create perceived power?*

5.4 TACTICS

It's key to remember that satisfaction, level of comfort and power are crucial elements in every negotiation. Some of these elements will be more applicable in certain negotiations than others. I'll explain more about this in the next chapters.

As you will have experienced, many buyers will apply tactics to win negotiations. Tactics will always contain one of the three elements mentioned above. Just remember that tactics are never personal; they exist to win the negotiations game. Still today, some buyers use the same tactic over and over again, since it has worked for them in the past. These buyers need a little reminder to change up their ways of working.

A supplier had a payment issue with one of their customers. This was not just any customer but a major account and were therefore treated with the utmost care by the supplier. The issue was that the customer's procurement team refused to pay for services they asked the supplier for beyond contractual commitments. This wasn't a one-time issue, it happened frequently.

All the supplier wanted was to get paid for the extra service they provided to the customer. The fact was that the supplier felt so powerless in the relationship that it was impacting their personal life for months. Perhaps they felt powerless, but were they truly powerless?

After a closer look, it turned out that the customer had pressures too. At the end of every month, the customer's sales targets had to be met. This was a crucial target since it impacted the bonus scheme of every single employee. The solution was actually quite simple; here is what the supplier said to the customer:

'If you don't pay the open invoices, we will immediately go back to our contractually agreed service levels'

The customer was consciously asking a lot more than what was contractually agreed upon. The supplier knew that going back to the agreed service levels would significantly impact the customer's sales targets, something the customer was not willing to accept.

This one sentence meant that the discussion was completed within two days and, within a week, all invoices were paid. Every discussion between the customer and supplier went smoother from that point forward. All they needed was a reminder of who was actually in power in the relationship.

► *Q16. In their negotiations with you, is customer x mainly focused on satisfaction, comfort or power?*
► *Q17. What exactly do they do that makes you draw that conclusion?*

6. Negotiation chairs and tables

6.1 NEGOTIATION CHAIRS

Think about your last face-to-face negotiation. It is highly likely that you were sitting on a chair next to a table. Typically, buyers and sellers find themselves on each side of the table. Interestingly, this confirms the perception of a conflict. Now, you can sit on two types of chairs during negotiations: a blue chair or a red chair. These pictures explain the difference:

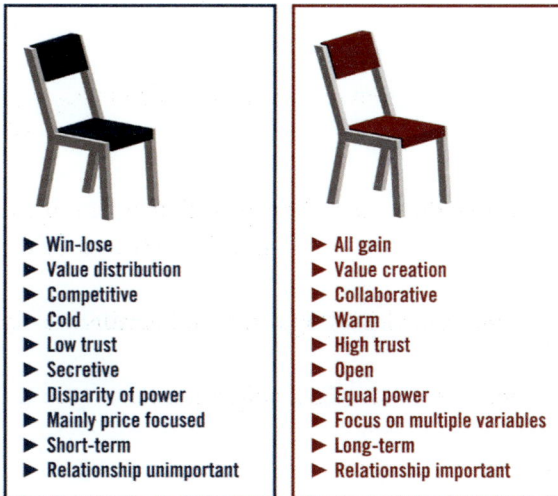

▶ Win-lose
▶ Value distribution
▶ Competitive
▶ Cold
▶ Low trust
▶ Secretive
▶ Disparity of power
▶ Mainly price focused
▶ Short-term
▶ Relationship unimportant

▶ All gain
▶ Value creation
▶ Collaborative
▶ Warm
▶ High trust
▶ Open
▶ Equal power
▶ Focus on multiple variables
▶ Long-term
▶ Relationship important

Figure 6.1 Negotiation chairs

An example of a blue chair would be when you buy or sell something on eBay. Generally speaking, it will be a one-off purchase. As a buyer, you want to pay the lowest price and, as a seller, get as much for it as possible. On the other side, engaging in a long-term strategic partnership is a red chair negotiation. You want to ensure successful cooperation continues after the negotiation. An example is a negotiation you have with your partner or kids. Trust me, this is red chair!

In real life, chairs will never be entirely red or blue; there is a large spectrum in between. However, for the purpose of taking an effective approach to negotiation, it's best to consider it one or the other. When linking the colour of the chair to an organisation's procurement maturity, you can draw the following conclusions:

✓ Companies operating at operational level: the customer is typically on a red chair.
✓ Companies operating at tactical level: the customer is very often on a blue chair.
✓ Companies operating at strategic level: the customer can be either on a blue or red chair depending on what works best for them in each particular situation.

▶ *Q18. Based on the answer you gave to Q8, what is the colour of the chair customer x is sitting on?*

When taking a look at the three fundamentals of negotiation combined with the colour of the chair, you can assume the following:

✓ Customers focusing mainly on satisfaction: it is highly likely they are sitting on a red chair.
✓ Customers focusing mainly on power: it is highly likely they are sitting on a blue chair.
✓ Customers focusing on comfort: they could be sitting on either a blue or a red chair depending on how subtle or extreme they are in their approach.

► *Q19. Based on the answer you gave to Q16, what is the colour of the chair customer x is sitting on when negotiating with you?*

► *Q20. Based on the answers to Q18 and Q19 as well as your personal experience, do you think customer x is sitting on a red chair or on a blue chair when negotiating with you?*

► *Q21. What is the colour of the chair <u>you</u> are sitting on when negotiating with customer x?*

6.2 NEGOTIATION TABLES

The colour of the negotiation table is determined by the colour of both negotiation chairs. This means there are three possible combinations:

1. Both chairs are blue
2. Both chairs are red
3. One chair is blue and one chair is red

6.2.1 BLUE CHAIR + BLUE CHAIR = BLUE TABLE

When both chairs are blue, the colour of the table will be blue as well. A straight-forward example of this would be when you buy a carpet at a bazaar. You want to pay as little as possible and the seller wants to receive as much money as possible. These are opposing objectives with a strong focus on the price and little focus on the relationship. The best way to win the negotiation is by using (perceived) power.

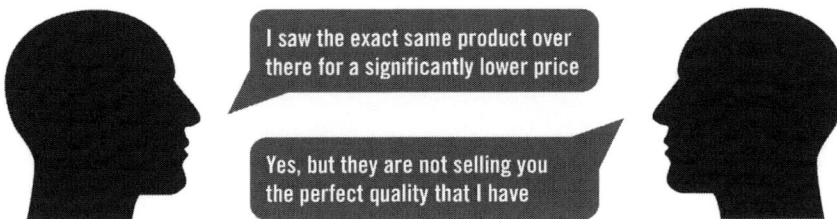

Figure 6.2 Sentences used in a typical blue table conversation

Do you recognise what's happening in this picture? Both parties are trying to create perceived power. The buyer shows they have other options to buy and the seller tries to create a situation where they are the only one selling this particular quality.

Power is very strongly linked to having options. The more options you have, the more power you have in negotiations. This is called BATNA; **B**est **A**lternative **T**o a **N**egotiated **A**greement. A complex acronym for having a plan B. When you have an alternative, it will make you feel more powerful because you know exactly when to walk away from a deal. So, the key to winning at the blue table is by having and/or creating more perceived power than the other party.

6.2.2 RED CHAIR + RED CHAIR = RED TABLE

When both chairs are red, the colour of the table is red too. This is a recipe for a long and hopefully fruitful relationship. Typically, in these situations there is an equal balance of power. If that isn't the case, there is a risk of the party with more power taking advantage and turning their chair blue at some point in time.

So, what to do when the table is red? Red table negotiations are about creating value together. How can we both benefit from this relationship? It starts with asking questions and giving information. You need to know what the other party wants and the other party needs to know what you want. Obviously, the key word is trust here. Without trust, you cannot engage in a long-term relationship. Once you both know what you and the other party want, you can start to make mutually beneficial proposals. The focus here is to:

Give the other party what they want ... under your conditions

Consider this example: a major customer said the following to one of its suppliers: 'Over the last year we have grown our business by 3% which means we have grown your business by 3% as well. For this, I want you to pay us $10 million'. By replying 'That is outrageous, I will never do that', you turn both chairs, and thus the table, blue.

Instead, you could reply with, 'If you give us guaranteed sales of $200 million and exclusivity in all your stores, we are happy to pay you $10 million'. Now, you're giving the other party what they want…under your conditions. The value you gain from this deal is worth more than the $10 million they ask for, and as a result, you are staying at the red table while negotiating.

There are three key insights here are:

1. Always take <u>when</u> you give. If you only give something, it will build greed with the other party and you'll risk making their chair blue. For example, when you negotiate with somebody and you ask for a 2% discount and the other party accepts, what will you do next time you meet this person? Exactly! Ask for more. The reason is simple: since this was so easy to obtain, there must be more to gain. Remember that satisfaction is low if you accept straight away.
2. Always take <u>more</u> than you give. The idea is that every proposal you put on the table should make it better for you. No matter how extreme the request from the other party is, you should ask for more value than you give them.
3. Always ask <u>before</u> you give. By using 'If you…, then I…', you ensure that your proposal is conditional and that you ask something before you give something to the other party. This is important because people stop listening to you once you give them something first. Compare the following two examples:

Example 1:
A: 'I can give you 60 days payment terms….'
B: 'Great, thank you. Much appreciated.'
A: 'Sorry, actually I wasn't finished yet with my proposal…'

Example 2:
A: 'If you accept a price of 100, then I can give you 60 days payment terms'
B: 'Thank you for your proposal.'

6.2.3 BLUE CHAIR + RED CHAIR = BLUE TABLE

When one party is blue and the other party is red, you will be negotiating at the blue table. This means that the one sitting on the blue chair will take advantage of the one sitting on the red chair. The red chair negotiator is willing to invest in a long-term relationship, whereas the one on the blue chair is looking to making an easy win. The result will be:

RED will be giving and BLUE will be taking

At the risk of generalisation, sales people are often red chair negotiators. They want to invest in the relationship and grow the business together with the customer. Buyers are typically blue chair negotiators. The reason for this is that most procurement organisations have a tactical operating maturity which means a strong focus on the results through rigorous tendering processes. They want to ensure they get the best deal now as this will help them to achieve their functional objectives.

As a matter of fact, if you think about customer x right now, there is a high likelihood that you are sitting on a red chair and they are sitting on a blue chair. Without a doubt, this is the most challenging of the three situations to deal with. The good news is: there is hope. You now moved from unconsciously incompetent to consciously incompetent, which is the first step to becoming (un)consciously competent. So, here's what you can do under these circumstances:

1. Change to a blue chair yourself as well and accept that you are negotiating at the blue table. To do this, you need to find ways to gain power in the relationship. Think about the pressures the other party has and how you can use those to your benefit. Remember, it's about changing the perceived balance of power in your favour.
2. Try to get the other person to sit on a red chair and create a red table negotiation. Typically, this is a bit harder to do. If the other party believes they have more power, they are more likely to want to stay blue. Therefore, you need to find a way to show that you are of equal power and that working

together is more beneficial to both of you. Yes, sometimes it does require to get to the blue table first before you can start building a red table together.

During the next chapters, we'll go into more detail on how to do this. The colour of the chairs and table is always a snapshot in time; things are susceptible to change, often driven by changing circumstances. One company faced this challenge with a key supplier:

A customer had been working with a supplier for many years. They had a good mutual relationship and business was going well for both. At one point, the economy weakened resulting in declining financial results for the customer. In an attempt to protect their profits for the year, the customer put pressure on the supplier to meet their prices and threatened to move their business elsewhere. All of a sudden, the colour of the chair changed from red to blue and thus did the table. Just like that!

▶ *Q22. Based on your answers to Q20 and Q21, at what colour table are you negotiating with customer x?*
▶ *Q23. Based on the colour of the table, what is going to be your negotiation strategy going forward?*

7. Know your buyer

7.1 THE SPEND TREE

When a buyer steps into their role, one of the first things they do is analyse the total spend of the categories they are responsible for. The best way to do this is through a spend tree which is basically a segmentation of a buyer's total spend into smaller categories.

Once completed, the buyer will first focus on spend. The highest spend categories are the ones of most interest to buyers, since this is where they can make the biggest impact and demonstrate the added value they deliver. Secondly, a buyer will take a look at the risk areas. The ones where there is a risk of supply or quality are of particular interest. In practice, most buyers will approach these risk areas reactively, only to solve an issue when there is one, rather than pro-actively.

In the example of the spend tree on page 55, 'road transport' and 'market warehousing' would be high on the buyer's radar because they represent more than 50% of their total spend. Alternatively, 'customer deliveries' could be important too since quality and service are crucial here, and any issues they have could directly impact the company's sales targets. The focus here would be to manage the risks associated with this area.

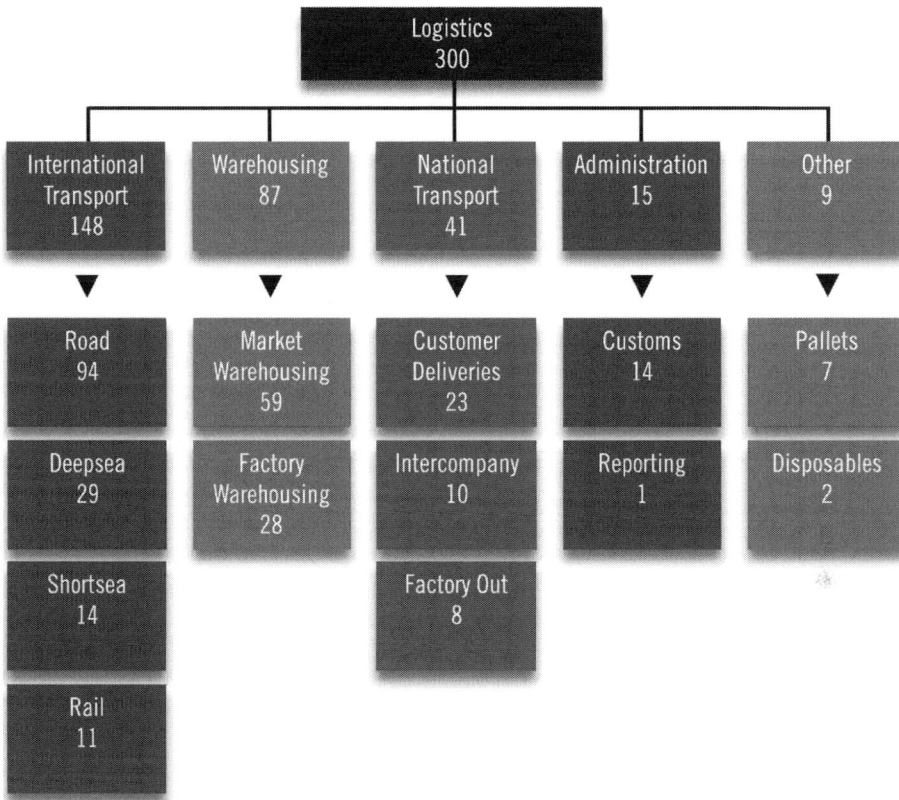

Figure 7.1 Example of a spend tree (in million $) for logistics costs of a large multinational

Obviously the spend tree can be expanded, for example, under market warehousing, where a further split could be made into handling and storage. However, the objective is not to split to the highest level of detail, but to split into the levels at which the market operates. In this specific example, there is a market for 'market warehousing' and not for 'handling'. From this perspective, you could also argue that road, short sea and rail are one and the same, since they compete for the same business. While this could be true, it depends on the bigger picture. If companies have sustainability targets to reduce CO_2 emissions, then separating these markets makes sense.

As a sales professional, it's necessary to understand how important you are to a buyer because that determines the amount of time they are willing to invest in you.

▶ *Q24. Which categories is customer x responsible for buying? What is customer x's total spend or budget in all categories they buy? (if you don't know exactly, an estimate is fine)*
▶ *Q25. What does customer x spend on the category you provide products or services in? Therefore, how important is this particular category for customer x?*

7.2 THE COMPETITION

Generally speaking, a buyer's worst nightmare is to be 'single-sourced' on one or more of the categories they buy. Being single-sourced means that buyers have only one supplier to source their products or services from. This poses three major risks:

1. **Financial risk;** the buyer's negotiation position is weak as there is no possible alternative. The balance of power is clearly in favour of the supplier who can use this to improve their financial position.
2. **Service risk;** what if the supplier's factory shuts down due to a power failure, and they are unable to deliver products to the buyer's company? What will the buyer do? How do they keep their own factory running?
3. **Quality risk;** what if the supplier has a quality incident? What is the buyer going to do then? Buy bad quality products or stop their production completely? Hardly a choice, is it?

Some buyers believe in the concept of single-sourcing as it allows them to strengthen the relationship with their supplier. While it can be mutually beneficial, as soon as the balance of power shifts, you are exposed to the three risks mentioned above. The same applies for 'force majeure' situations which are not controlled by the supplier such as strikes, natural disasters, etc.

In 2000, a fire at a microchip plant in Albuquerque, New Mexico, USA affected supply to a large mobile phone manufacturer. The smoke and water damage contaminated millions of microchips. One mobile phone manufacturer had no alternative source of supply. They were forced to wait it out and hope for a better situation to come.

The situation wasn't resolved quickly and this disaster cost that mobile phone company $400 million in lost sales. To make things worse, they had to quit the mobile phone business due to months of lost production. The competition did have alternative microchip sources and was now able to dominate the mobile phone market.

Buyers love to have a choice with regard to the suppliers they work with so they will go to great lengths to ensure there is a level of competition in the market. In order for a buyer to assess the competition, they will take three perspectives to suppliers in a specific market:

1. **Current suppliers;** these are suppliers they can source from within a short period of time, either because they are already working with them or they have been approved in the past.
2. **Alternative suppliers;** these suppliers could be up and running within one year. Though this is not a short-term option, these suppliers are worth investing in to ensure competition in the near future.
3. **Non-traditional suppliers;** these suppliers could be available within a period of one to three years, since they require investment in service, quality and/or capital. Nevertheless, they could be of interest in the future and therefore should be monitored on a six-month basis.

When buyers run tenders, they will typically invite both current and alternative suppliers. Even though they cannot actually award business to alternative suppliers, they are relevant to identify potential savings opportunities for next year's tender. That determines whether they are worth investing time in now.

► *Q26. Based on your answer to Q4 and Q5, do you know who your competitors are for customer x (current/ alternative/ non-traditional)?*

7.3 KRALJIC' PURCHASING PORTFOLIO MATRIX

If you would ask a professional buyer what the most important model in procurement is, around 90% would choose Kraljic' purchasing portfolio matrix. The other 10% would either be ignorant or lying to you about it. This matrix was created in 1983 by Peter Kraljic, a former director at McKinsey. Still today, it is one of the most widely used tools in procurement, and for good reason.

Supply Risk

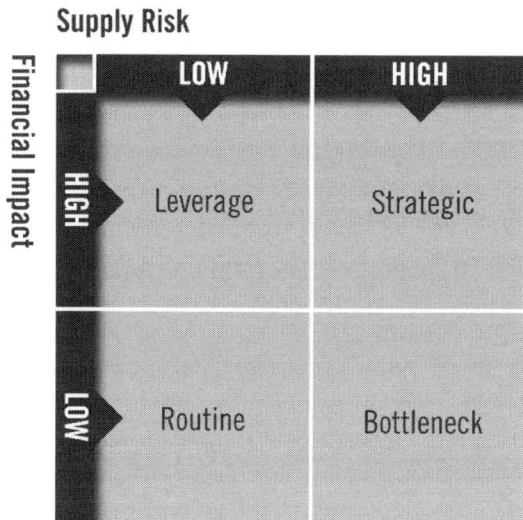

Figure 7.2 Kraljic' purchasing portfolio matrix

On the horizontal axis of the model, you'll see 'Supply Risk'. There are three questions that provide guidance to assess the actual risk:

1. Is there enough availability of these products or services on the market? Yes/No
2. Is there more than one supplier capable of delivering the product or service you require? Yes/No
3. Is it easy to switch suppliers? Yes/No

If any of these questions is answered with 'No', then the Supply Risk is high. In all other cases, the Supply Risk is low.

> Imagine you are buying pens. There are hundreds of potential suppliers, so the supply risk is low. But what if you're buying a specialist piece of machinery and there is only one supplier capable of delivering the required specification? In the latter case, the supply risk is high.

On the vertical axis, you can find 'Financial Impact'. This is best described as the impact of the sourced product or service on the profitability of the final product.

> When you're buying cleaning services for offices, the financial impact will typically be low. However, when you're buying pulp paper and you're working in the cardboard packaging business, one can assume the financial impact is high since that cost represents a significant chunk of your company's spend and therefore profitability.

7.3.1 THE BUYER'S STRATEGY

Each of the four boxes represents a corresponding strategy:

1. **Routine;** low financial impact, low supply risk. The strategy is to minimise efforts through long-term contracts, optimising order volume and inventory levels. A buyer doesn't want to spend time and energy on this since it has little business impact.
Example of routine: office stationery. You can buy stationery at low cost almost anywhere you want.

2. **Leverage;** high financial impact, low supply risk. The best strategy is to leverage the market by using purchasing power and tools such as tendering and auctioning. Buyers love being here since this is where they can contribute the most.
Example of leverage: transportation in the Fast-Moving Consumer Goods (FMCG) industry. There are hundreds of suppliers of logistics services, and typically transport represents a large chunk of a FMCG company's spend.

3. **Bottleneck;** low financial impact, high supply risk. The strategy here is to minimise risks. The two most common ways to do this are as follows:
A. Through supplier approvals. By creating alternative supply options, buyers reduce the risk of non-supply.
B. By decomplexifying the specification. By changing the specification from customer specific to industry standard, buyers open the door to other potential suppliers and as such reduce the risk of non-supply.
Example of bottleneck: specialist software. Even though it can be expensive, for most corporations it will rarely have a significant impact on their total spend. Due to the fact that it's specialist software, there are no other suppliers available for this.

4. **Strategic;** high financial impact, high supply risk. The best strategy is to develop long-term relationships with suppliers, analysing and managing risks regularly. This is best done through strategic alignment meetings.
Example of strategic: Boeing/Airbus engines for an airline operator.

Even though there are some suppliers in the market, there is typically only one or maybe two suppliers capable of delivering engines for a specific aircraft. It goes without saying that the financial impact of these engines is high.

It is imperative to consider this model for each market individually. Even within the same industry, there can be multiple markets.

In the example of the factory needing coarse sugar, the market was 'bottleneck' since there was only one supplier capable of delivering the specification and the financial impact was low, with only a relatively small surcharge for sieving.

Once the specification changed to industry standard, and the market became global, the strategy changed to 'leverage'. As a result of the change, the global market opened up and due to the large influx of suppliers, there was a significant opportunity for cost savings and increased profitability.

When you struggle to define which of the four boxes you are in with your customer, it often helps to consider the buyer's behaviour with regard to strategy. Are they interested in working together or not at all? Are they giving you a lot of attention and focus or not really?

In general, buyers like to be in a position of power and will therefore always aim to reduce their risks (move to the left side of the model). They don't like being in a position where they can only source from one supplier. Despite not liking it, this doesn't mean they actually have the power to change it because that often requires cross-functional teamwork.

A buyer's behaviour should only be used as an indication, since it can be misleading, too. For example, when buyers 'leverage' the market by running a tender, you can be pretty sure that at least some of the products or services they are sourcing are in 'bottleneck'. The key take-away is that you should always consider your own information. Don't be fooled by a buyer's ability to create perceived power.

7.3.2 THE BUYER'S CHAIR

If we now create an additional layer of insight to Kraljic' matrix by adding a red or blue chair to each of these boxes, the result would look like this:

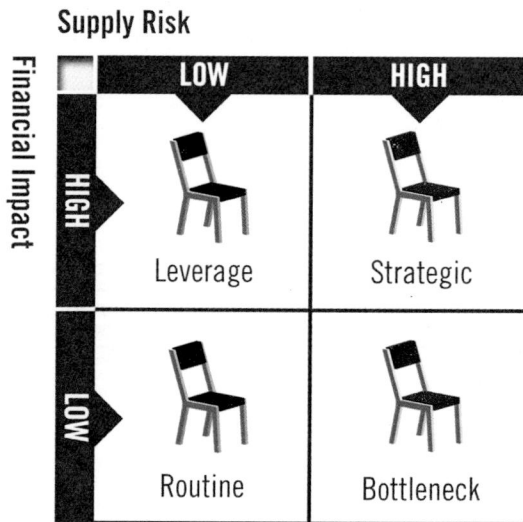

Figure 7.3 Kraljic' purchasing portfolio matrix including red/blue chairs

In a high supply risk situation where there are few suppliers, the buyer has to sit on a red chair since they are dependent on the other party. In the case of a low supply risk situation, a buyer can sit on a blue chair since there are many other parties to source from.

We're now bringing the answers to the questions in Chapter 7 together.

▶ *Q27. Based on the answers you gave to Q24 and Q25, do you believe the financial impact of the category you provide products or services in to be low (a small percentage of total spend) or high (a large percentage of total spend) for customer x?*

▶ *Q28. Based on your answer to Q26, do you believe the supply risk is low (many competitors) or high (no or few competitors)?*

▶ *Q29. Based on your answers to Q27 and Q28, which box in Kraljic' matrix are you currently in? Does the corresponding strategy match how customer x is acting when dealing with you?*

▶ *Q30. In an ideal world, which box in Kraljic' matrix would you like to be in with customer x? Why?*

8. Know yourself

As a seller, of course, you have a perspective on your customer too. How do you see your customers and how does it drive the decisions you make? Rather than focusing on the emotional aspect, let's take a logical approach to this by using the supplier preferencing matrix.

8.1 SUPPLIER PREFERENCING MATRIX

This tool is used by buyers to assess how they believe suppliers see them. It's always an assessment of a buyer's perspective and that means it does not necessarily correspond to reality. If you reverse this thinking pattern, it can be an ideal tool for sellers to explain how they see their customers. By taking a two-step approach, you will understand how to behave towards your customer, and more importantly, why you do it that way.

On the horizontal axis of the model, you will find 'Dependency'. Here, you're assessing your customer's dependency on you. Practically, this means it's about understanding how many options your customer has to source from an other supplier. If, for a specific market, you're the only one capable of supplying to a certain customer, dependency is high. If there are many others in the same market that could potentially supply to this customer, dependency is low.

Dependency

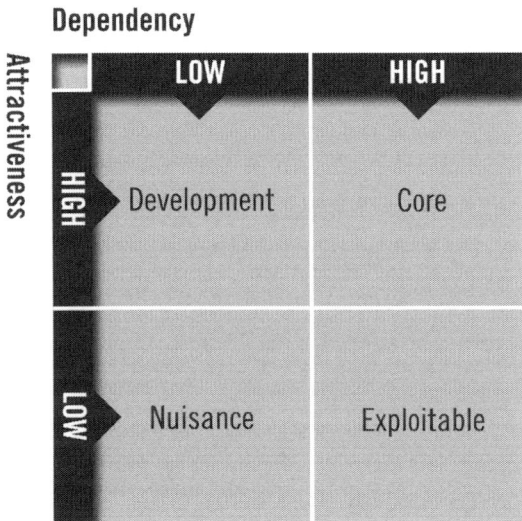

Figure 8.1 Supplier preferencing matrix

A customer needs a bespoke raw material to manufacture a branded product that is in high demand. This particular raw material is patented by one of its suppliers and cannot be sourced anywhere else. Dependency is high in this situation.

On the vertical axis of the model, you will find 'Attractiveness'. Often buyers assume this is linked to the name of their company:

'I work for a big company so I'm attractive for suppliers'

Even though this can be the case, it's more likely that attractiveness is linked to the seller's functional objectives such as potential growth, profit margin, or even the ease of doing business. A buyer will therefore be perceived accordingly:

'You're attractive because I think I can grow my business with you'

A supplier of household products is working with a retail customer for the sales of soaps and other cleaning products. They have been working together for a year now and the retail customer has shown interest in the supplier's portfolio of detergents. This is a significant business opportunity that could help secure the supplier's growth objectives. The customer is therefore perceived as highly attractive with regard to the supplier preferencing matrix.

8.1.1 THE SELLER'S STRATEGY

Each of the four boxes represents a corresponding strategy:

1. **Nuisance;** low dependency, low attractiveness. You give low attention to, and show little interest in, the customer. You could lose the customer without pain.
   Example: a small-time contractor buying construction materials from a large do-it-yourself store.
2. **Exploitable;** high dependency, low attractiveness. You have an opportunity to maximise profit. The customer is dependent on you since you have the power in the relationship.
   Example: A highly specialised technology consultant working for a small business owner in need of their services.
3. **Development;** low dependency, high attractiveness. You will nurture the customer and seek opportunities to expand the business. Ensure pro-active service to keep the customer satisfied.
   Example: A manufacturer of packaging material has set up a new production facility. They are participating in a large regional packaging tender for a global A-brand business.

4. **Core;** high dependency, high attractiveness. Ideally, you have a strategic partnership with your customer. You will fight to keep the account through high levels of service and responsiveness.
   Example: A supplier of car engines is preferred supplier to a large car manufacturer.

It's imperative you consider this matrix for each individual customer. Every customer in every market deserves their own position within it.

The management teams of both a supplier and customer had top-to-top meetings to discuss strategy, long-term partnerships and more. One day, it was announced that the supplier acquired its biggest competitor, also a supplier to the customer, and therefore the customer became 70% dependent on this 'new' supplier. The supplier was obviously aware of this level of dependency because it took them less than a week to send a message to the customer: 'From next week on, all your prices will increase by 20% or we will stop delivering our products to you.' Within a week, the customer moved from 'core' to 'exploitable'. Just like that!

Why did they lose attractiveness in such a short amount of time? Since dependency increased to 70%, attractiveness therefore dropped because the customer wasn't as profitable for the supplier and there was no room to grow the business anymore. Knowing that 70% dependency is not a long-term sustainable solution and that the customer would seek to reduce their dependency by finding alternative suppliers, the supplier decided to exploit the customer in the short-term.

Changing circumstances meant that the strategy moved from 'core' to 'exploitable' in a very short period of time.

8.1.2 THE SELLER'S CHAIR

Now we'll add an additional layer of insight to the supplier preferencing matrix by adding a red or blue chair to each of these boxes. The result looks like this:

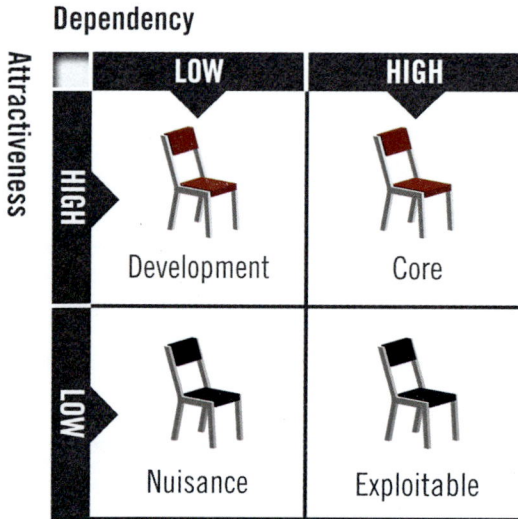

Figure 8.2 Supplier preferencing matrix including red/blue chairs

When you work with an attractive customer, you're in it for the long run and so you have to sit on a red chair. When they are less attractive to work with, you can sit on a blue chair because you won't mind if you stop working with them.

Do you recognise that buyers tend to be good at pretending they are attractive? They like to show, there is potential to do business in the future or make promises to improve day-to-day operations. The simple reason is that if a seller finds a customer attractive to work with, the seller sits on a red chair and is therefore willing to invest in the relationship. For a buyer, a red chair seller is so much better than a blue chair seller. Just compare the words 'nuisance/exploitable' to 'development/core' and you'll notice the difference.

- ▶ *Q31. How attractive is customer x? Why is customer x perhaps not attractive?*
- ▶ *Q32. How dependent is customer x on you? Are there alternative suppliers they could work with?*
- ▶ *Q33. Based on your answers to Q31 and Q32, what box in the supplier perception matrix is customer x currently in?*
- ▶ *Q34. In an ideal world, what box in the supplier preferencing matrix would you like to see customer x in? Why?*

9. The Power- Balance matrix

Now we're bringing it all together: the chairs, the table, Kraljic' purchasing portfolio matrix and the supplier preferencing matrix. We're transforming this into one new model called the Power-Balance Matrix. As the name suggests, this matrix will show whether one party has more power than the other, or whether the power is balanced between both of them.

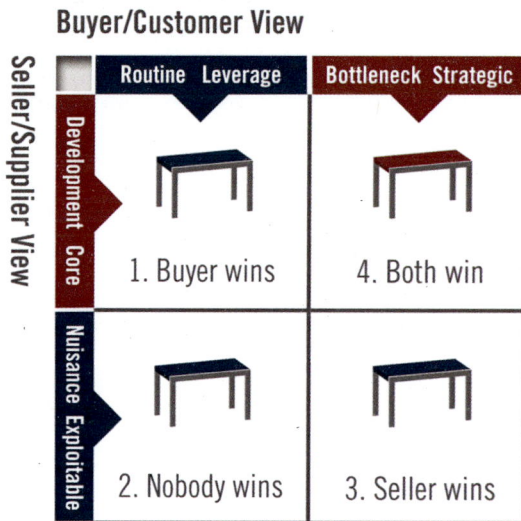

Figure 9.1 The Power-Balance matrix

The Power-Balance matrix is created by combining the results from Kraljic' purchasing portfolio matrix on the horizontal axis and the supplier preferencing matrix on the vertical axis. The colour of the table in each quadrant depends on the colour of the chairs on each axis. Every market-supplier combination deserves its own place in the matrix. If a supplier is operating in different markets, then each market should be assessed individually. The same applies for multiple suppliers in the same market. They all deserve a spot in this matrix.

1. **Buyer wins;** the buyer sees the current market as a place with plenty of suppliers so they are interested in getting the best deal, whereas the supplier wants to invest in the relationship with the customer. They are sitting on a blue chair, you are sitting on a red chair and, therefore, the table is blue. This means the buyer will take advantage of you and win in negotiations. You'll be giving and they'll be taking.
2. **Nobody wins;** the buyer wants to find the best possible deal in the marketplace and the customer is not very attractive to you either. Both of you are sitting on a blue chair and, therefore, the table is blue as well. Nobody really wins in these types of situations.
3. **Seller wins;** the buyer has limited suppliers to work with and you are not very interested in working with them unless it is beneficial to you. The buyer is sitting on a red chair, you are sitting on a blue chair and, therefore, the table is blue as well. This means you can take advantage of the situation and win in negotiations.
4. **Both win;** the buyer doesn't have a lot of options and you value the customer as well. Both of you are sitting on a red chair and, therefore, the table is red as well. Ideally, you work together in partnership. If done well, both should win in negotiations.

There is not enough arable land in China to grow the amount of sugar needed to meet rising demand. This means China is dependent on the supply from sugar exporting countries such as Thailand or Brazil.

In order to control the sugar market, the Chinese government has set base prices for sugar beet and cane, which means sugar buyers have little to negotiate with suppliers except processing and logistics costs. As a result, the market can be considered 'bottleneck'. There is a high 'Supply Risk' due to the general shortage and limited 'Financial Impact' due to governmental price setting.

Company Y is sourcing sugar for the production of beverages in Guangzhou, China. They are working with a large supplier who is delivering 55% of the total volume requirements. Company Y is an important customer since they are instrumental in supporting the supplier to uphold their leading quality standards. From this perspective, the customer is perceived as 'Core', high 'Attractiveness', as they support their supplier on improving their quality standards, and high 'Dependency', as they buy 55% of their volume from 1 supplier.

Combined, 'Bottleneck' and 'Core' means that they are in box 4. Both win. In this case, both customer and supplier are ideally positioned to be working together on a strategic partnership that benefits them both.

▶ *Q35. Combining your answers to Q29 and Q33, what is your current position in the Power-Balance matrix?*
▶ *Q36. Combining your answers to Q30 and Q34, what is your ideal position in the Power-Balance matrix? Why?*

10. Strategies for success

Based on the assessment in Chapter 9, it's now time for the 'how-to'. Knowing what box in the Power-Balance matrix you're currently in and knowing where you'd ideally like to be, means that we can now look at what you need to do to get there. Each box will have one or more corresponding strategies. Some of them with a focus on the short-term, others on the long-term. It's up to you to determine what works best for your individual situation.

✓ Box 1 – 'Buyer wins' will be discussed in paragraph 10.1
✓ Box 2 – 'Nobody wins' will be discussed in paragraph 10.2
✓ Box 3 – 'Seller wins' will be discussed in paragraph 10.3
✓ Box 4 – 'Both win' will be discussed in paragraph 10.4

Depending on your answer to *Q35*, select the corresponding paragraph to find out what action(s) you could take.

10.1 BUYER WINS

As a seller, this is probably one of the worst boxes to be in. Nevertheless, half the value is in knowing that this is where you are. There are a couple of things you can do here, some are quick to implement, others require long-term actions.

A customer is buying logistic services and they organise a yearly conference for their transport providers creating an opportunity to discuss improvements in their ways of working. Even though palletised transport is a classic example of a 'leverage' market, the customer was investing time, money and energy in remaining attractive for its suppliers. The reason for this was that it ensured that the suppliers remained on a red chair whereas the buyer was sitting on a blue chair. This meant that the buyer would always win in tenders and negotiations.

The fact is that the buyer is in a position of power and ideally, you'd like to change that. You are interested in a long-term relationship with this customer whereas they are not since they have plenty of other suppliers to choose from. They are leveraging the market through tenders and you're investing time in the relationship hoping to win some business at the mercy of the customer. Now that we've set the scene, here's what you can do in these circumstances:

10.1.1 SHORT-TERM ACTIONS

Short-term means, anything you can do to prepare for the upcoming negotiations you have with this customer. They are in a position of power so it's imperative to ask yourself a couple of questions before you go into a negotiation with them:

✓ What if we cannot get to a deal? What is my alternative?
✓ When do I walk away from the deal? What is the minimum I can accept?
✓ Is my plan aligned with senior internal stakeholders?

You have to bear in mind that the other party is looking to get the most out of you because if you don't play ball, someone else will. Since the best tools for buyers are to leverage the market through tenders and auctions, there is a risk that you keep lowering your prices in order to secure the business. Sellers don't like to lose customers since it impacts their year-end sales targets. So, when a buyer puts pressure on to you, what do you do?

1. Lower your price to keep the customer, or
2. Stick to your price and lose the customer

These are the only two options you have and it feels like you have to choose between the lesser of two evils. As such, always know what your limits are and align them with internal stakeholders. The risk if you don't is that you get to a deal which is unfavourable for your business either in terms of lost sales (losing the customer) or financial loss (accepting too low prices which impacts profitability). Come prepared with what you can and can't do!

10.1.2 LONG-TERM ACTIONS

If you don't change the situation you are in, you will be 'leveraged for eternity'. Remember the following quote from Darwin:

'It is not the strongest of the species that survives, nor the most intelligent that survives. It is the one that is most adaptable to change'

This leaves you with several options that will help you escape the position you are in. This list of four options is not exclusive, but it should be enough to trigger your creativity toward a strategic action plan:

1. Redesign your product or service proposition
2. Bypass the buyer
3. Buy the competition
4. Become the cost leader

OPTION 1 REDESIGN YOUR PRODUCT OR SERVICE PROPOSITION

Currently there are many other competitors just like you so the question is: what can you do to become unique again? This requires you to rethink and change the product or service you are offering to your customers. Some examples of this are:

✓ Changing the functionalities of your product or service
✓ Entering a niche market through specialisation
✓ Premiumisation of service, product or packaging
✓ New Product Development

A mushroom farmer found herself surrounded by hundreds of competitors and, as a result, prices were under constant pressure. They were being leveraged by the wholesale industry and several competitors eventually went bust.

One day, this particular farmer decided to invest in sustainability. After a couple of years of hard work, she became the first ever carbon-neutral producer of mushrooms in the world. At one point in time, even the biggest retailer in the region wanted to go into business with her because carbon-neutral mushrooms supported their sustainability targets.

This farmer moved from 'routine' to 'bottleneck' by making her product unique again.

▶ *Q37. What can you do to differentiate your products or services from your competitors? How can you become unique again?*

OPTION 2 BYPASS THE BUYER

By showing you can add value to other functions besides procurement, you can gain direct access to a business. For example, become a thought leader on a specific topic. A thought leader is an individual or company that is recognised as an authority in a specialised area. By using that expertise, you can gain access to other functions in companies, ideally bypassing the procurement teams.

Another option would be 'value-based selling'. This process focuses on first identifying the issue the customer has and then on the value you have to offer to them. By showing functions, other than procurement, what personally tailored, unique value proposition you have to offer, you gain access to an organisation before the traditional procurement gatekeeper steps in.

One specific customer works with the 'DFV-principle' for innovations to fuel their growth ambitions.

D = Desirability (does the customer/consumer want this?)
F = Feasibility (is it technically possible to make?)
V = Viability (is it financially attractive to make?)

A well-known and trusted supplier supported this customer by getting involved at an early stage of the design process. Their expertise helped to ensure that the feasibility and viability of the product was thoroughly checked and approved before going to market. As a result, the customer was extremely pleased that they were able to manage the process from an idea to the launch over a shorter timescale. As a positive side-effect, the supplier was able to influence the design and specification of the product, making themselves indispensable.

▶ *Q38. What do you have to offer on thought leadership or value-based selling? How can you use this to get a seat at the customer's table?*

OPTION 3 BUY THE COMPETITION

A more drastic approach would be to buy the competition. In the field of technology, this is common practice:

✓ Facebook acquired Messenger, WhatsApp, Instagram and 80 odd other companies
✓ Google acquired DoubleClick, YouTube and over 200 other companies
✓ Microsoft acquired Yammer, Skype, LinkedIn and more than 200 other companies

A fundamental decision needs to be made whether to invest in scale-businesses (to increase market share) or in scope-businesses (to add a new scope to your business). The latter has actually become more popular in recent years.

▶ *Q39. What competing businesses could you buy?*

OPTION 4 BECOME THE COST LEADER

In this situation, you accept that you are in a 'leverage' market and you have no intention of pursuing options 1, 2 or 3. If you want to survive in this market, you need to become the cost leader to guarantee you your business in the future. The only way to achieve this is through rigorous cost-cutting and by achieving efficiency gains to stay ahead of your competition. One way of doing that is by setting up a cross-functional team led by a program manager dedicated to explore and execute cost saving opportunities.

▶ *Q40. What do you need to do to become the cost leader in your market?*

All in all, this is one of the most challenging places to be. The reason for this is that it is hard work to get out of the buyer-wins-situation. Particularly because you cannot do this alone and you need a team of people from different functions within your own organisation to support you on this journey.

10.2 NOBODY WINS

You don't care. They don't care. Who cares? Actually, nobody cares.

You are in a 'routine' or 'leverage' market so there are many competitors for the buyer to source from. At the same time, the customer is not really of interest to you, either. The strategy here is as straightforward as can be. If the deal is not beneficial to you, just walk away. That's it. There is no more to it. Just make sure you know exactly what you can and cannot do before going into negotiations. The way to do this is by understanding your limits since the customer will be looking for the best possible deal. If the customer eventually decides to work with you, it probably means you have provided them with the best possible price.

Over the long-term, the thing to remember is, situations can change. Even though neither of you is currently interested in the other, you never know how this may change in the future.

10.3 SELLER WINS

Now it gets to be interesting for you. This is where the balance of power is in your favour and the key question for you to think about is: how am I going to use my position? Are you going to increase your prices? Are you going to leverage your influence to secure additional business? The options are only limited by your imagination. In order to streamline your thoughts, remember the following:

With great power comes great responsibility

You now have the power in the relationship and, depending on how you use it, you can expect a different response from the buyer.

A customer was using a highly specialised law firm for specific services. The law firm knew that the customer had nowhere else to go since there were no other providers on the market capable of delivering the service like they could. They decided to ask for a 10% price increase on their hourly rates.

The customer had to accept. Nonetheless, they were not pleased. Therefore, they started to establish a working relationship with other law firms who were looking to enter this particular niche market. Even though these law firms were not capable of delivering the full service, the customer did eventually manage to move 40% of the total volume of work to other law firms hoping to develop capable long-term suppliers and create permanent competition in the future.

Buyers don't like to be put in corners and will fight hard to get out, especially if the financial impact is high. So, what does that mean? Does that mean you cannot use your power in these kinds of situations? Absolutely not, simply that you need to evaluate the consequences of your decisions thoroughly.

Over the short-term, you can pretty much get away with anything. I mean, what other option does your customer have? So, the key question is not linked to the short-term, but to the long-term: what are the long-term consequences for using power in the relationship? As mentioned, a buyer will look for any opportunity to change the situation. Determine therefore how likely it is that a buyer will actually take steps to do so.

The best model to use for this evaluation is called Porter's Five Forces. The model originates from Michael E. Porter's 1980 book 'Competitive Strategy: Techniques for Analyzing Industries and Competitors'. It's a powerful tool that can be used for understanding the competitiveness of your business environment.

Figure 10.1 Porter's Five Forces

The model is based on the idea that there are five forces at play that can have an impact on the profitability of your business. Each force needs to be assessed individually with low, medium or high for your particular business. These five forces will be explained by using the airline industry as an example:

1. **Threat of new entrants:** How quick and easy is it for new joiners to enter the market?
   Example: high investments, infrastructure and government regulation make it difficult, yet in the past years several mainly low-cost airlines have succeeded in joining. Rating: medium

2. **Threat of substitutes:** How easily can your product/service be substituted?
   Example: for business travel virtual meetings and other technology is proving a threat reducing the need for travel. Example: for private travel this typically concerns holidays or family visits. Trains, boats/ cruises, cars, or holiday close to home are potential substitutes for air travel. Rating: medium

3. **Supplier power:** How much power do your suppliers have?
   Example: there are only two suppliers of aircrafts in the world (Airbus and Boeing). Rating: high
   Side note: there are of course other suppliers to the airline industry such as, but not limited to, fuel (low), labour (low), government taxes (high) and airports (high).

4. **Buyer power:** How much power do the buyers of this product/service have?
   Example: customers can choose between many airline service providers, especially on the more common destinations. Rating: high

5. **Competitive rivalry:** How strong is the competition in the market?
   Example: this is due to many service providers and low-cost airlines that operate in the market. Prices have been under pressure year-after-year. Rating: high

The more you have rated a force as high, the more likely it is that you can lose the preferential position you are in. It is therefore unwise to use too much power in the relationship with your customer since it can backfire later.

In the airline example, there are two mediums and three highs, which means the industry is under constant financial pressure. Traditional airlines have been losing market share to low cost airlines, leading to industry consolidation of the traditional airline operators as well as various bankruptcies.

On the other hand, the more you have rated low on these five forces, the stronger your position is as a seller and the harder it will be for the buyer to replace you. In other words, the more lows, the more you can exploit your customer because they have nowhere else to go now and that is unlikely to change in the future. Obviously, there is a limit to how far you should take this. There are always risks associated with using your power, such as:

✓ **Reputational damage, impacting other or future business**
   Example: for Facebook, all five forces are low which means they have a lot of power. News events about privacy and data leaks are great examples of the reputational damage they have sustained, leading to a global decline in users.

✓ **Pushing a profitable customer into financial difficulty or even bankruptcy**
   Example: in the retail market, for products such as clothing, household appliances, toys, etc., the rise of the internet led to numerous bankruptcies amongst shops and retail chains. Manufacturers used internet sales as an opportunity to expand businesses which led to the demise of the traditional retail industry whose cost base was significantly higher than that of internet shops.

✓ **Investors could decide to enter the market when they learn how profitable your business is**
   Example: patents in the pharmaceutical industry are a great example of copycat behaviour due to the low cost and high profit margin. The development process of a new drug can take decades, however, once it's proven to be successful, it's relatively easy to copy.

Having power is great since it gives you options. However, it is always important to assess the long-term consequences of these decisions.

▶ *Q41. How would you assess Porter's five forces for the market you operate in?*
▶ *Q42. As a result, what are the risks for exploiting your customer over the long term?*

10.4 BOTH WIN

This is a great position to be in for both parties since it can generate mutual value. Basically, you both need each other and that need should be acknowledged by both of you. That said, it doesn't come easy because it requires trust, understanding and openness. The basis for this is to make sure both parties are aligned to the idea that working together is the best way forward for both of you. Unfortunately, there are many factors that could stop you from going on this journey together, such as:

✓ Our bosses expect us to put pressure on the other party to win the negotiation
✓ Company culture; 'we have never done this before'
✓ Senior management does not want me to spend time on this currently
✓ Lack of trust that this process will deliver anything beneficial
✓ Etc.

You need to take away these hurdles for both companies if you want to pursue this path. Find advocates and educate stakeholders about why this is beneficial for your company. You now have access to the following tools to support you in this discussion:

✓ Red/blue chair and table
✓ Kraljic' purchasing portfolio matrix
✓ Supplier preferencing matrix
✓ Power-Balance matrix

Once you've managed to align the organisation behind your intentions to drive value for both parties, you're left with two options: a short-term and a long-term approach. Needless to say, the long-term approach has a much more sustainable outcome (horizon of 1 year and more), however it requires more time and energy from both parties. The short-term approach is very useful for upcoming negotiations (horizon of 1-12 months).

10.4.1 SHORT-TERM APPROACH

For the short-term approach, the structure to use is diamond-shaped. The core is shiny and beautiful (red table). However, you also need to be aware of the sharp edge at the bottom, the conflicting objectives (blue table). The key is not to cut yourself with this, but to focus both parties on the shiny, shared objectives in the center. This is the place where you can get the most value. Have a look below:

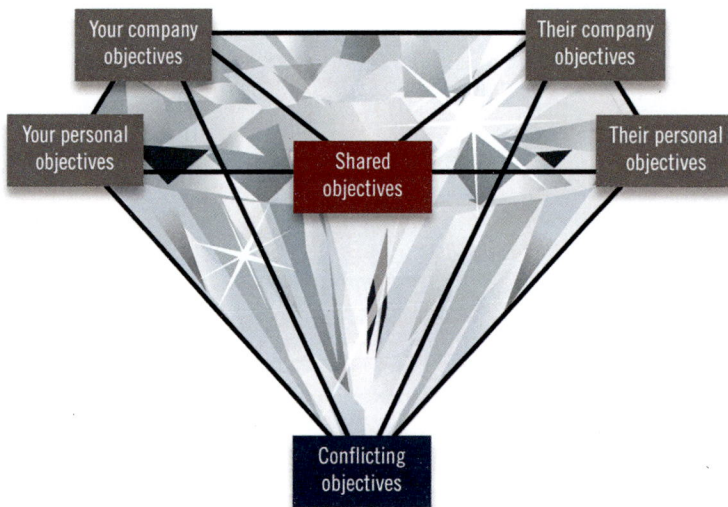

Figure 10.2 Objectives diamond

You complete this objectives diamond by means of a three-step assessment:

1. Assess your company and the other company's objectives.
2. Translate these objectives into your personal objectives and the personal objectives of the buyer opposite of you.
3. Assess which areas are shared objectives (red table) and which are conflicting objectives (blue table).

A supplier of a highly specialised raw material has signed a five-year contract with a large manufacturer of products for the animal feed industry. This could be the start of an even larger opportunity to work together as both parties are interested in a long-term partnership. Both parties have an interest to grow the business since this will create higher revenues and profits. The aim is to secure growth by improving quality as well as new product development.

The buyer is particularly interested in lower prices to ensure their business can remain competitive in the industry. The seller, on the other hand, is interested in shorter payment terms since this allows them to use cash for investing in expanding their production capacity. The shared objectives are to grow their respective businesses. Their conflicting objectives are costs versus payment terms.

Once you have completed this assessment, there will be several objectives in the red box and several in the blue box. It's now crucial to start bringing these together since you both want to be at the red table, now and in the future. This means the objectives in the red box are aligned so there is no need to focus there, other than to confirm the benefits of working together. Instead, you need to focus on the objectives in the blue box since you need to find an agreement on this.

The best way to negotiate these objectives is to first assess the importance of each objective for both parties. The importance can be low, medium or high, and it can be evaluated based on the value or cost for both you and the other party. Once you have evaluated all objectives for both parties, it's time to categorise them according to the conditional trading matrix:

Importance For Them

	LOW	MEDIUM	HIGH
LOW	No conflict	Give	Give
MEDIUM	Take	Minor area of conflict	Give
HIGH	Take	Take	Area of conflict

(Vertical label: Importance For You)

Figure 10.3 Conditional trading matrix

There are five different boxes in the conditional trading matrix:

1. Three red boxes that state 'Take'. These are the objectives you want to take as they are more important to you than to the other party.
2. Three red boxes that state 'Give'. These are the objectives you want to give since they are more important to the other party than they are to you.
3. One grey box that states 'No conflict'. In red table discussions, topics of low importance to both parties are not worth fighting over.
4. One blue box that states 'Minor area of conflict'. Since these are equally important to both of you, this is considered the sharp edge of the diamond.
5. One blue box that states 'Area of conflict'. This is a real challenge and sharp edge since this is of high importance to both of you.

Now it's time to start making proposals. The best way to do this is by trading conditionally. As we've learned, conditional trading means you never give away anything without asking for something in return. Remember the golden rule: always ask for something of higher importance to you (one of the three 'Take' boxes) and give something of higher importance to them (one of the three 'Give' boxes). As explained in chapter 6.2.2, the best way to make conditional proposals at the red table, is by using:

'If you ..., then I ...'

The animal feed manufacturer could make proposals to the supplier such as:

✓   'If you give me a price of $100 per tonne, then I can give you 60-day payment terms.'

✓   'If you give me a price of $98 per tonne, then I can give you 15-day payment terms.'

Remember, at the red table, always...

✓ **Take and Give**
✓ **Take before you Give**
✓ **Take more than you Give**

When you are discussing the objectives in the blue boxes (the two blue areas of conflict), consider the following ideas to keep the table red throughout the negotiation:

✓ Think creatively. Perhaps you can cut the variables into smaller pieces, focus on small differences in objectives, use timing in the discussion or add additional variables into the mix. It pays to listen attentively and clarify when unclear.

✓ Save the areas of conflict for the last part of the negotiation. By agreeing on all other topics first, it will be easier for both parties to close the last part of the negotiation. Sometimes this means compromising to support both your higher objectives.

✓ If there are too many high-high objectives, you might want to reconsider whether you're actually negotiating at the red table. Perhaps it's blue after all. And if this is the case, your approach should be different as explained in chapter 6.2.1.

For short-term negotiations, go through the following steps:

▶ *Q43. List each objective in the blue box and assess the importance (low/medium/high) for you and the other party.*

▶ *Q44. Place each objective in the conditional trading matrix.*

▶ *Q45. Based on the conditional trading matrix, what proposals can you make to move to a mutual agreement?*

10.4.2 LONG-TERM APPROACH

In case you wish to establish a long-term relationship with your customer and they wish to as well, you need to intensify the connection. It's exactly like in a marriage; it's about finding the right balance to make it work together and sometimes that means one of you needs to make a sacrifice for the benefit of the other.

So, how do you create a lasting relationship with the other party? This is not something that is simply created overnight, it requires a rigorous and structured process focused on making deep connections, both personally and professionally. This journey is not to be underestimated. To facilitate that process, I will guide you through the pre-work and the five fundamental steps that will help you to create this level of connection. By following these steps, you'll have a recipe for success for a lasting relationship with your customer.

In order to start building the connection, it's important both parties meet together. My experience has shown that it is best to organise a two-day off-site meeting with representatives from both companies.

PRE-WORK

There are a couple of things that need your attention before you jump into this joint working session.

Firstly, people from various functions from both organisations should join the workshop, not just the buyers or sellers. Ideally, for each invitee a counter-part from the other company should be present. For example, you would like a customer service representative to connect with the supplier's inbound logistics coordinator, or the supplier's raw material expert to meet with the customer's quality and food safety professional. Bridges are built at every level in the organisation and the more bridges you build, the stronger the relationship becomes.

That said, don't invite more than five people per organisation to avoid endless discussions and only invite decision makers to the meeting. It doesn't help if someone says, 'I need to check that', throughout the meeting.
You also need to have a facilitator to guide you through. This person can be employed by one of the companies. However, it's imperative that this person is as neutral as can be so they can challenge both companies and not treat one preferentially. To safeguard neutrality, you could decide to hire someone externally.

Pre-work checklist:
✓ Supplier team set up and engaged
✓ Customer team set up and engaged
✓ Two-day off-site location booked
✓ Facilitator appointed and prepared

Once the pre-work is done, it's time to participate in the workshop. Participants don't need to prepare anything for this since the results will flow naturally by following the process. Just make sure you have invited experts in their respective fields to the meeting.

As mentioned, there are five steps for a successful process which will be detailed below:

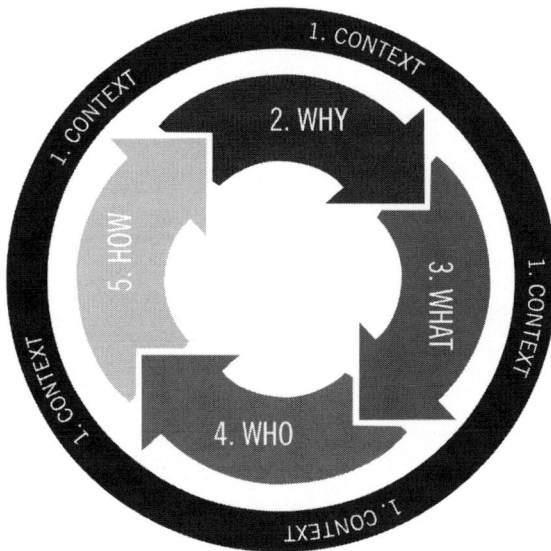

Figure 10.4 The 5 steps for building a lasting supplier-customer relationship

STEP 1. CONTEXT

As you can see, Step 1. Context is placed outside the inner circle. It's important that you create a joint picture of the current reality you are both in. This is the bigger picture of your existing relationship which requires you to recognise that you both might have a different starting point. The best way to bring two teams together is to get to know each other better and to build personal as well as business connections. It's as you can see in the figure 10.5:

Figure 10.5 The importance of context

If everyone would be looking from their own perspective (from within one of the nine boxes above), they would all miss the fact that they are looking at an elephant. Only by bringing everyone together will you be able to identify the 'elephant in the room'.

In this phase, we are particularly interested in all perspectives on the current relationship. We need to look from the same starting position in the same direction for the partnership to be a success. In order to do so, there are some important questions that need to be answered by the participants. There are three questions to understand the context of the business both parties are in, and three personal questions to build bridges at individual level.

The three business questions:
1. Why does your business exist?
2. How would you describe its culture and beliefs?
3. What are the current challenges your business faces?

The three personal questions:

1. What three words would friends/family use to describe you?
2. What are your personal beliefs and values?
3. What would be your ideal outcome today?

The purpose of this exercise is to get to the core of each individual and identify as many commonalities as possible. It shows that people and businesses are not that different after all. The insight that we are all the same automatically builds a connection between people.

STEP 2. WHY

Now that you've got all the noses are pointing in the same direction and people are clearer about the others in the room, as well as the business context, it's time to ask ourselves: 'Why are we a team?' If people don't understand why they are in the room, they will tune out very quickly.

> I received an invitation for a meeting to discuss a new product launch. Assuming they wanted to know more about the procurement of the ingredients, I accepted and joined the meeting. The meeting turned out to be about technical specifications and I had no clue why I was even invited. I found myself catching up on my e-mail while everyone else was discussing the topic at hand.

We've probably all experienced a similar situation and it's true: once you're unsure <u>why</u> you are in a meeting, you lose interest. It's human nature. This affirms the importance of ensuring you invite the right people to the workshop. To facilitate ensuring that everyone in the room is clear about why they are brought together, there are four questions that need to be answered:

1. Why must this team work interdependently?
2. What unique value can we bring together?
3. What is the legacy we want to leave as a team?

4. What would our key stakeholders say our purpose is?

These four questions should fuel a discussion to create a joint purpose statement. A purpose statement is a compelling reason why a group must work together to create value and why it matters. It anchors attendees to a shared identity and it focuses them on where they add unique value.

A number of conditions must be met for a purpose statement to work. The analogy I use here is tomato SAUCE. A good tomato sauce contains certain ingredients: tomato, olive oil, onions, parsley and salt/pepper. Without these ingredients, it just doesn't taste as great as it should. Here's a description of what SAUCE stands for:

✓ **Short** - Concise/Brief/Crisp/Simple
✓ **Aspirational** - Hopeful/Appreciative/Future-focused
✓ **Unique** - Original/Differentiating/Distinctive
✓ **Catchy** - Sticky/Clever/Memorable
✓ **Every Day** - Useful/Practical/Consistent

Figure 10.6 SAUCE of a purpose statement

All five boxes (Short – Aspirational – Unique - Catchy - Every day) need to be ticked to have an outstanding purpose statement.

One example of using this process was when I was working at my previous employer. I decided to test this method with a packaging supplier. Up to that point, we had rarely created a true partnership with a supplier so it was an eye-opening experience for all of us.

We went through a two-day workshop and the entire first day was spent on context and creating a common purpose. I originally assumed it would be a waste of time, but in hindsight it was an extremely powerful start. We came out as a strong team and I still look back positively on that experience and the connections we built.

The initial objective of the workshop was to identify saving opportunities by working closely together. For us, it meant lower costs. For the supplier, it meant securing long-term business since it would significantly improve their competitiveness in tenders. At the end of the first day, we created the following purpose statement:

TOGETHER we
drive efficiency by
breaking through
the **complexity** of the
world of **packaging**

Figure 10.7 Team's purpose statement (FMCG industry and packaging supplier)

The initial results after the workshop were phenomenal. By using the supplier's expertise, we were able to make our packaging design process much more efficient resulting in significant financial benefit.

The pitfall during this process is that people focus too much on the WHAT instead of the WHY. An easy way to ensure you get it right is by remembering that the WHY focuses more on the emotional part, whereas the WHAT is more logical. At the end of the WHY process, you can, for the first time, call the group a team. You now have something that binds you: a common purpose.

Nike is a company that has created a powerful purpose statement with their 'Just Do It' slogan. It ticks all of the SAUCE-boxes, for that matter. Nike lives by its purpose by tackling controversial social themes. Marketing their purpose as they do almost always results in a rise in sales for them.

STEP 3. WHAT

Next up is the WHAT. Once you have identified the WHY, the WHAT tends to flow naturally from it. During this step, the team decides WHAT three big rocks they will focus on going forward. The following process helps you to create team consensus on the three big rocks:

Figure 10.8 The 3 big rocks

✓ Each individual team member writes down what they believe the team should focus on going forward. Use one post-it per idea and restrict ideas to three per person.
✓ Each individual shares their ideas with the group.
✓ At the end, group the post it notes to identify the top team priorities.
✓ Discuss each priority and decide through consensus which are the top three.

If you find that the group agrees on two or four priorities, do not worry; as long as you have identified the big rocks and not the pebbles, you are in fine shape.

In the previous example with the packaging supplier, we wanted to focus on cost reductions by thinking differently than before. Therefore, we identified the following three big rocks:

1. What can we do to further optimise the current specification?
2. What parameters are key to a fit-for-purpose packaging specification?
3. What does the ideal packaging development process look like?

Each of these big rocks helped deliver our common purpose. We took three different perspectives on improving the current packaging process and each of them contributed toward that goal.

STEP 4. WHO

The next step is to define WHO will be doing WHAT. This means cutting the big rocks into digestible deliverables and creating an action plan for each one. To facilitate this, the entire group is split into three working groups, one working group per big rock. Ensure there is a good mix of expertise and companies per working group. Each working group completes their 'big rock worksheet'. Use the following tips to ensure high quality output from this process:

✓ 'From/To' defines where you are now and where you want to go to. What does success look like for this particular big rock?

✓ All individual deliverables should add up to the total big rock.

✓ Plan 'working sessions' including timing, team members and make sure to assign a lead. This will help you to set a deadline, to track progress and to ensure each deliverable is realistic to achieve.

As soon as the working groups complete the big rock worksheet, they each present it to the full team. The full team can, in turn, add comments to each big rock worksheet to ensure everyone approves it.

Big Rock:		Overall Lead:	
From: To:			
Deliverable:	Working Session:	Timing:	Team: (bold = lead)

Figure 10.9 Example of a big rock worksheet

A couple of 'watch-outs' for this process:

✓ Ensure timing goals are realistic. Most people have day-to-day jobs to execute next to this project, so don't expect delivery of all actions within a week. However, it's important to keep focus on timely delivery as well. Balance is key.

✓ Every workshop member should have one or more actions since it's a team project plan and everyone should be included.

✓ Make sure you don't allocate a large part of the actions to the same person as this will jeopardise the process going forward.

At the end of this process, an overall project lead should be appointed to lead the entire project. This means you will have three different kind of leads each with a clearly defined role:

1. Overall project lead – accountable for the overall project
2. Big rock project leads – accountable for delivery of each big rock
3. Deliverable leads – accountable for each deliverable

STEP 5. HOW

Now that all actions and owners have been agreed to, it's time to agree on HOW you will work together as a team in the future. In order to do so, there are at least three different meetings and meeting rhythms that need to be agreed to:

1. The full team led by the overall project lead.
2. The big rock teams led by the big rock project leads.
3. The key stakeholders led by the overall project lead.

For each of these meetings, a couple of decisions need to be made:

✓ Who are the participants? (At a minimum all action owners)
✓ What is the frequency? (Ideally fixed day and time)
✓ What is the meeting medium? (Face-to-face or virtual)

By involving everyone in a correct manner, you ensure engagement levels are high throughout the project. Ultimately, this increases the chance of success.

FINALLY

As a team, you have now created a fantastic opportunity for working together. It's important to remember that situations change and so will the content of what you have agreed to. Remain flexible to work with changing circumstances such as a team member leaving their role or deadlines that become unrealistic for whatever reason. Consider the fact that the team is going on a journey. Value the connections you have built as this will help you overcome the challenges you face. It's important to keep in mind that you enjoy the ride together…

'If you want to go fast, go alone.
If you want to go far, go together'
– African proverb –

▶ *Q46. Do you think it's possible to go on this journey with customer x?*
▶ *Q47. What steps are you going to take to create this opportunity?*

11. The journey ahead

Wow, you did it! You took the first steps toward dealing with your most challenging customer. The most important step to running a marathon is the first, and you just completed it. However, by now you will understand that the journey doesn't end here. So far, it has been a lot of theory and now it's time to put it all into practice. The best way to do that is through structured action planning.

11.1 ACTION PLANNING

Go through all the notes you've made and questions you've answered through the book and identify up to five actions you are going to take after you have completed reading this book. Be specific on what the actions are and by when you intend to complete them. At the bottom of the action plan, you'll find a section to enter your name, the current date and your signature. These sections are there to help you make a commitment to yourself and stay accountable.

As a final step, make sure you plan time in your calendar to execute the actions you've planned. This helps you to meet the timelines you have indicated in your action plan.

WHAT	BY WHEN
A	
B	
C	
D	
E	
Name: Date: Signature:	

Figure 11.1 Action plan

11.2 THE SIX KEY STEPS

The relationship between a buyer and a seller can be troublesome because that is sometimes the nature of the role both parties are in. It is hard to truly understand the other party all the time even though you aim to do your utmost. And you know what? That's ok; it remains a learning process you need to go through with each buyer you meet. It is unrealistic to expect to be perfect. If it were easy, everybody would have mastered it by now. And as you've read buying-selling started 3,000 B.C. and it's still a difficult process more than 5,000 years later. Don't worry, you'll get there. By every time following these six key steps, you will get to a better result when dealing with your customers:

Step 1. Understand a buyer's objectives (BCG-matrix, purchasing maturity, the importance of procurement in an organisation).

Step 2. Determine current and future position in Kraljic' purchasing portfolio matrix (the buyer's view).

Step 3.   Determine current and future position in the supplier preferencing matrix (seller's view).

Step 4.   Assess current and future position in the Power-Balance matrix (combined view).

Step 5.   Define your corresponding strategy moving from current to future.

Step 6.   Create and execute your action plan.

Below you will find an example case in which the six steps are taken.

A supplier of co-packing is providing two services to one of its key customers:

✓   Re-casing; repacking factory cases to display cases.
✓   Pouch-filling; bespoke packaging line for filling pouches with liquid food.

Step 1. Understand a buyer's objective
✓   All products that need to be re-cased can be classified as stars due to increasing demand, whereas pouch filling is a new activity and is considered a question mark according to the BCG-matrix.
✓   From a purchasing maturity perspective, the customer is strategic. They are open to various options in terms of dealing with their suppliers such as tendering and long-term partnerships.
✓   The procurement team reports directly into the CEO and the buyer therefore has three key objectives: support growth ambitions, deliver value for money and ensure continuous supply to customers.

Step 2. Kraljic' purchasing portfolio matrix
✓   Re-casing is a large spend category for the customer and there are many other co-packers capable of delivering this service.
    Re-casing can therefore be classified as a 'leverage' category.

✓   Pouch-filling is a new activity and currently only a small fraction of the customer's spend. There are not many co-packers capable of delivering this service due to the relative high investment costs. Pouch-filling can be classified as 'bottleneck'.

Step 3. Supplier preferencing matrix
✓   The supplier is seeing many growth opportunities with the customer since they outsource a lot of their activities to co-packers. This means the customer is attractive from a supplier's perspective. Furthermore, at this stage, the customer is not dependent on supplier. The supplier sees the customer as 'development'.

Step 4. Power-Balance matrix
✓   Re-casing fits into box 1. Buyer wins. The buyer has a range of suppliers to choose from and will leverage the market for the best possible deal.
✓   Pouch-filling fits into box 4. Both win. In this situation, both parties have a mutual interest to make this a success together.

Step 5. Defining your strategy
✓   For re-casing, the supplier decides to become cost leader by partly automating the re-casing line. By reducing the impact of manual labour, the supplier can decrease production costs. As a result, their competitiveness in the market improves.
✓   For pouch-filling, the supplier decides to organise a joint-strategy session with supplier. By building stronger connections, both parties hope to improve quality, cost and service levels. At the same time, the supplier sees this as an investment in the relationship with the aim to continue to grow the business together.

Step 6. Action plan
✓ For re-casing, a project team is created including a employee from the customer to investigate the long-term viability and feasibility of various cost-saving initiatives.
✓ For pouch-filling, an external facilitator is hired for a two-day workshop leading to a joint project plan.

11.3 TWO FINAL QUESTIONS

Before this book comes to an end, I'd like to ask you to have a look at your answers to the questions *Q2* and *Q3*. Do you believe they have been answered? Do you feel more empowered to deal with customer x? Whether your answer is 'Yes' or 'No', I invite you to share your thoughts and any questions you might have. Visit my website at www.roi-10.com, connect with me via LinkedIn or send me an email at info@roi-10.com. I'd love to hear from you.

That's it. You're ready to go back into the world and make a difference. Good luck, I hope you have a great journey!

Index

List of questions